Three Months with

PAUL

Three Months with

PAUL

Justo L. González

ABINGDON PRESS

Nashville

THREE MONTHS WITH PAUL

Originally published as *Tres meses en la escuela de la prisión:
Estudios sobre Filipenses, Colosenses, Filemón y Efesios,* copyright 1997

English translation copyright © 2006 by Abingdon Press

This book is printed on acid-free, elemental-chlorine–free paper.

Library of Congress Cataloging-in-Publication Data

González, Justo L.
   [Tres meses en la escuela de la prisión. English]
   Three months with Paul / Justo L. González.
     p. cm.
   ISBN 0-687-49539-3 (binding: pbk., adhesive : alk. paper)
   1. Bible. N.T. Philippians—Devotional literature. 2. Bible. N.T.
Colossians—Devotional literature. 3. Bible. N.T. Philemon—Devotional litera-
ture. 4. Bible. N.T. Ephesians—Devotional literature. I. Title.

BS2705.54.G6613 2006
227'.06—dc22
                                          2006003322

06 07 08 09 10 11 12 13 14 15—10 9 8 7 6 5 4 3 2 1

MANUFACTURED IN THE UNITED STATES OF AMERICA

C O N T E N T S

INTRODUCTION

This book is an invitation to study and to adventure. As a study it will require discipline. As an adventure, it will offer new panoramas and exciting challenges.

Let us address discipline. Every important goal in life requires a discipline. If a young person wishes to become, for instance, a doctor or a lawyer, it will be necessary to follow from an early age a discipline of study and learning. If we are concerned about our physical health, we try to follow a discipline of exercise and nutrition. Athletes who prepare to compete in the Olympics must subject themselves to a rigid discipline for years on end. And yet, when it comes to spiritual life, very few Christians are willing to subject themselves to a discipline that will develop and strengthen it. With the excuse that we should "pray without ceasing," we do not set aside a particular time for prayer. And, since the Bible is always there, ready to be opened and read whenever we need it, we do not set a program of study. The result is that both our prayer and our knowledge of the Bible suffer, just as the body suffers when instead of following an ordered diet and a discipline of exercise we eat whatever strikes our fancy and exercise only when we feel like it.

The first thing that we need in order to develop a discipline of study is to set aside a time and a place. The studies in this book follow a weekly rhythm: Each week there will be six short studies and a longer one. If you then follow this study privately, you will require at least half an hour a day for the six short studies and an hour for the longer one. Consider your weekly calendar and decide the best time for you to set aside for study. Once you have done this, make every possible effort to fulfill that commitment. Little by little, just as it happens with physical

exercise, that study rhythm will become more and more important for you, and the time will come when, if for some reason
you are not able to follow it, you will feel the need for it.

If you are using this book as part of a Bible study group that
gathers once a week, establish your rhythm of study so that the
six shorter sessions take place on the days that you study in private, and the longer one on the day the group meets.

On the other hand, don't be too idealistic regarding the time
you have set aside for study. Life always has its unexpected
interruptions, and therefore very few people are able to follow a
discipline of study without interruption. Sooner or later the day
will come when it will be impossible for you to study during the
time that you have set aside. In that case, do not be disheartened. That very day, even if at another time, try to study the
material assigned for it.

A place for study is almost as important as a time. To the
extent possible, have a particular place where you normally do
your private study. This will help you avoid distractions. It will
also be a convenient place for you to keep your Bible, this book,
your notebook of personal reflections, and any other material
that you may find useful.

The next important point in developing a discipline of Bible
study is the method one follows. There are many good methods
for the study of Scripture. The one that we shall follow in this
book consists of three fundamental steps: **See, Judge,** and **Act.**

However, before we discuss these three steps, there are two
important elements that must be stressed, without which no
Bible study can be productive: prayer and reflection.

At the very moment you begin each study, approach God in
prayer. Ask that the Holy Spirit be with you during this study,
helping you understand God's Word, and that the Spirit remain
with you after you have completed the session, helping you to
follow what you have decided. Always remember that, even
though you seem to be by yourself, you are not alone; God is
right there with you. It is not just a matter of you and your Bible,
but rather of you, your Bible, and the Holy Spirit.

After a few minutes of prayer, devote some time to reflection, reviewing what you have studied before. In particular, remember those decisions you have made on previous days. Read your notebook. Evaluate what you have accomplished. Ask God for the strength to go forward.

Move then to the three steps of **seeing, judging,** and **acting.** As you will note, the material offered under each study is organized according to those three steps. The first, **seeing,** consists in examining the situation before you. In the case of these Bible studies, seeing will involve examining the passage itself. What does it say? Why does it say it? Who are the main characters? What role do they play in the text? What is the context of what is said? In this first stage, we are not asking what the text might mean for ourselves, or what it requires of us. We are only trying to understand the passage itself.

The second step, **judging,** consists of asking ourselves what the text might mean for us. Here, our personal experiences and our concrete situation become very important. We read the Bible in the light of those experiences and that situation, and ask what the Bible says about them. Therefore, when this book invites you to judge, it does not mean for us to judge the biblical text, but rather to invite the text to help us judge our own life, situation, opportunities, and responsibilities. What does the text tell us about the church, about our faith, about our society? How does it affirm and support what we are doing and what we are? How does it question or correct it? What does the text call us to do or to be?

These first two steps lead to the third: **acting.** What we have seen in the biblical text, and the manner in which we judge that text refers to our reality, requires that we act in a specific manner. We do not study the Bible out of curiosity, but in order to be more obedient to God's will. Therefore, the process is incomplete if we are content with seeing and judging. If we are to be obedient, we must act.

Acting can take many diverse forms, depending both on the text and on our own situation. For instance, the study of a certain passage may lead us to greater commitment to the poor and the needy in our community. The study of another passage may call us to witness to our fellow workers. And a third passage may call us to greater faithfulness in our participation in Christian worship. Furthermore, acting does not always imply physical activity. In some cases, acting may consist in a further prayer of repentance. In other cases, it may be abandoning a prejudice we have. Sometimes the action to be taken may be very concrete and brief; for instance, calling someone whom we may have offended. In other cases, it may be a long-term decision; for instance, taking up a different career. But what is always true is that, if we really study the Bible in a spirit of obedience, the Word that comes from God's mouth will not return empty, but will accomplish that for which it was sent (Isaiah 55:11).

Sometimes you will find that there are more suggestions for action than you can possibly follow. Take them simply as what they are: suggestions. Don't feel compelled to do whatever the book suggests. But do feel compelled to respond to your study of the Bible by an act of obedience—whatever that may be.

It is important to remember that we do not read and study the Bible only to be informed, but also and above all to be formed. We do not read the Bible so much to learn something, as we read it to allow that something to shape our lives. Once again, the example of physical exercise fits the case. Whoever exercises, lifts weights not only to see how much she or he can lift (in order to be informed), but also, above all, to become stronger, to be able to lift greater weight (that is, to be *formed*). Likewise, our purpose in these Bible studies should be not only to learn something, to know the Bible better, but also to allow the Bible to shape us, to make us more in accord with the will of our Creator.

This implies that the method of seeing, judging, and acting should be more like a circle than like a straight line. What this means is that acting improves our seeing, so that in fact the method could be described as seeing, judging, acting, seeing, judging, acting, seeing, and so forth. Every Bible study that we complete, each action that we take, will make us better able to move on to the next study. In order to understand this, think about a traveler in a valley. In that valley, the traveler sees a dense forest, a road that climbs a hill, and the position of the sun. On the basis of what he **sees,** the traveler **judges** that he is not to try crossing the forest, but rather to follow the road. He also **judges,** on the basis of the position of the sun, in which direction he should go. Then he **acts**; he begins walking. Eventually he finds himself atop the hill, where he **sees** new views that allow him to **judge** the direction to be followed and invite him to act in a way that he could not have guessed when he was in the valley. Therefore, his **acting** took him to a new way of **seeing.** The same will be true in a Bible study. If we make progress, we shall see ever wider views, and therefore not only will our seeing and judging lead us to a more faithful acting, but also our acting will clarify our seeing and judging.

What resources will you need to follow these studies? First of all, the Bible itself. Sometimes you will be tempted to shorten the time of study by not reading the Bible, and reading only what this book says. The temptation will be even greater when the biblical passage is well known. It is important to resist that temptation. The purpose of this book is to help you in your study of the Bible, not to be a substitute for it. In the studies that follow, the Bible is quoted according to the New Revised Standard Version (NRSV). Therefore, if you use that version it will be easier to follow these studies. Naturally, if you have more time, you may wish to compare different versions to enrich your study. Some people following these studies have reported that they have used a Bible with large letters and wide margins, so that they could write notes and comments. That is up to you.

Second, use this book. Try to follow the rhythm of studies suggested, reading and studying each passage on the day assigned. We are too used to living life in a hurry. Instead of cooking a roast for five hours, we place it in the microwave for thirty minutes. Sometimes we want to do the same with our spiritual life. If it is good for us to do one of these Bible studies a day, why not go ahead and do them all at once? Here once again the example of physical exercise may be useful. If you try to do a month's worth of exercise in a single day, the results will be very different than if you establish a rhythm of exercise and stick to it. Likewise, if we wish the Bible to shape us, to strengthen and to nourish our spiritual life, it is necessary for us to establish a rhythm that we can continue in the long run.

Third, you will need a notebook in which to write down your reflections, resolutions, and experiences. Write in it, not only what is suggested in some of the studies in this book, but also anything that seems relevant to you. If something strikes your interest, but you cannot follow up on it at the time, make a note of it. Write your answers to the questions posed in the book. Make a note of your decisions, your doubts, your achievements, your failures. Use your notebook at the beginning of each study session, in the period set aside for reflection, in order to help you remember what you have learned and thought in the course of your three months of study of Paul's letters from prison.

Make sure that every time you begin a study session you have at hand all of these resources: your Bible, this book, your notebook, and a pencil or pen.

No other resources are absolutely necessary for these studies. But if you wish to study Paul's prison letters more deeply, there are other tools that you may find useful: (1) several versions of the Bible, in case you want to compare them; (2) a good commentary on these letters; (3) a dictionary of the Bible; (4) a biblical atlas. These resources will be particularly helpful if the seventh session of each week will be a group study, and you are responsible for leading the group.

Finally, do not forget two resources readily available to you that are absolutely indispensable for any good Bible study. The first is your own experience. Some of us have been told that when we study the Bible we should leave aside all our other concerns. Nothing could be further from the truth. The Bible is here to respond to our concerns, and therefore our experience and our situation in life help us understand the Bible and hear God's Word for us today. The second such resource is the community of faith. I have already pointed out that when you study the Bible you are not alone with your Bible; the Holy Spirit is also there. Now I must add that, in a very real sense, your faith community is also there. Paul's letters generally were written to be read out loud, in the gathering of the church. Therefore, when you read them, even though you may be alone, keep in mind the community of faith that surrounds and upholds you. Read them not only as God's Word for you, but also as God's Word for the church. That is why this book includes the longer Bible study each week: to encourage readers to use it in study groups. These groups may gather once a week, but during the other six days you will each know that the rest of the group is studying the same Bible passage.

I said at the beginning of this introduction that this book is an invitation both to study and to adventure. On this last point, it is best to say no more. Adventures are best when they are unexpected and surprising. Plunge then into the study of Paul's prison letters, knowing that at some point it will surprise you, but knowing and trusting also that, even in such surprises, God is already there ahead of you, waiting for you with open arms!

Introduction to This Study: *Paul's Epistles from Prison*

The New Testament books that we shall be studying are often joined under the general title "Paul's Epistles from Prison." They are given this name because apparently they were all written when Paul was in prison. The traditional view is that he wrote these letters during the two years that, according to Acts, he spent in Rome. Other scholars suggest that they were written while he was a prisoner in Caesarea (Acts 23:23–26:32). Still others speak of a possible imprisonment of Paul in Ephesus of which Acts says nothing. Although these debates are interesting, they have little to do with the message of these letters. No matter where they were written—Rome, Caesarea, or Ephesus— their message is clear. Therefore, in the weeks that follow we shall not be looking at the question of where Paul was when he wrote these letters. (Nor shall we be overly concerned with the authorship of Ephesians, which according to some scholars was written not by Paul but by one of his disciples. I am not entirely convinced by the arguments that Paul did not write Ephesians, and in any case there shall be little occasion here for us to study these matters.)

What is important in reading these letters is that, wherever he was, Paul was a prisoner. His future was uncertain. That future was in the hands of authorities who had not the least sympathy for Paul or his preaching. And yet, the attitude that permeates these letters is not of fear or mourning, but rather of joy and victory. Repeatedly we shall see Paul rejoicing, not because he is in prison, but in spite of it. Faith helps him overcome the direst situations and the most menacing threats. If this is all we learn from the study of these letters, it will be more than enough!

W E E K

ONE

First Day: Read Philippians 1:1-2.

See: The first three words of this letter may surprise us. The title of the letter says that it is "the letter of Paul to the Philippians." But now the letter itself tells us that it is from "Paul and Timothy." While reading the rest of the epistle, you will note that all of it is in the singular, as if written by one person. Paul repeatedly says "I," and there is no doubt that he is speaking for himself. But he sets out by joining his name to Timothy's.

Paul's reason for doing this is clear. Timothy had close relations with the church in Philippi, and Paul expected these bonds to grow and be strengthened. Perhaps he also wished to give more authority to his young co-worker. Therefore, instead of simply sending greetings from Timothy, Paul joined the two names, thus signaling that they were of the same mind and that, in a way, Timothy shared his authority.

One should also note that Paul here does not claim the title of "apostle." He simply says that both he and Timothy are "servants of Christ Jesus." Further on, Paul will speak about how Christians must be humble and share among themselves. He begins his letter by showing that humility and that sharing. (Note, however, that in Galatians 1:1, writing to a church where he has to assert his authority, Paul clearly declares that he is an apostle, "sent neither by human commission nor from human authorities, but through Jesus Christ and God the Father, who raised him from the dead.")

Judge: In many of our churches there are conflicts over issues of authority and titles. Someone gets upset because another did not show proper respect by calling him "reverend" or "doctor." A founding member of the church is disturbed that younger members are taking her old position of leadership. A Sunday school teacher is annoyed when a member of his class shows that she knows something that he does not.

What do you think would happen in such cases were we to follow Paul's example? That example would lead us in two directions. First, it would show us that, no matter what other title we might bear, there is none greater nor more important than being "servants of Christ Jesus." Second, those of us who have a measure of authority must share it with those who do not—or rather, with those who are not recognized as having authority. Concretely, veteran members of the church must allow newer members to share in the leadership, and pastors and laity must also share their authority.

Act: Since you have set time aside for a disciplined study of the Bible, you are probably a respected member of your church. Take a moment to think about how that respect is shown—for instance, you are asked to pray in public, your opinion is sought, and some of your work is mentioned from the pulpit.

Now take the time to think about other people in your congregation who should receive the same respect but do not. Consider how you can share the authority that is given to you, how the work of others may be received with the same gratitude as yours; in short, how you may follow the example of Paul in beginning his letter "Paul and Timothy."

Write down your reflections and most particularly your decisions. In a few days read again what you have written, to see how faithful you have been to your own resolves.

Second Day: Read Philippians 1:3-4.

See: Verse 3 begins with a verb that stands at the center of the whole epistle: giving thanks. The other dominant theme in the epistle appears in verse 4: joy. As we study this letter we shall repeatedly see these themes of gratitude and joy. Even when not mentioned explicitly, they are the main thrust and message of the letter.

Note furthermore that here Paul offers thanksgiving for the Philippians. One of the reasons this letter is so full of gratitude and joy is the close bond between Paul and his readers. For them Paul is thankful.

At the same time, Paul prays for them. His relationship with them is not limited to good feelings between him and them, but also includes prayer for these people who, though far away, are Paul's sisters and brothers in the faith.

And he prays "with joy." At other times it will be necessary to pray in anguish and tears, but in this particular case Paul can pray with joy because the Philippians, and all that God has done in and through them, are reasons to rejoice.

Judge: We truly say quite often that Christian joy is grounded in faith, in the fact that we know that Christ Jesus has already won the battle. But there are also other reasons for Christians to rejoice. We rejoice in the fellowship of those who are truly our sisters and brothers in the faith. Even while in prison, Paul can offer thanksgiving and pray with joy, not because his imprisonment is a light matter, but rather because his joy and gratitude are nourished by the love that binds him to the Philippians.

Some Christians seem to think that the gospel is only a matter of one's personal life, of one's private relationship with God, of one's faith. But in truth the Christian life is a matter of community, of a family of mutual support, so that we can offer thanksgiving for one another and joyfully pray for one another.

Sadly, too often what is experienced in our churches is quite different from that. There are members whose devotion seems exemplary but who are at war with others. Brother X cannot stand Sister Y. Sister Z speaks ill of someone else. One group supports the pastor, and the other tries to make her life as difficult as possible. And we each think that we are holier than the rest, as if such attitudes and actions were of no more consequence than a sport or pastime.

The cost is very high. We lose the joy of which Paul speaks. We can no longer offer thanksgiving for one another. Now, even when we pray for others, we do it in bitterness, not joy. And then we wonder why the world does not believe!

Act: In your private notebook of reflections, where you will be the only person to see it, make a list of those people in your church or community whom you cannot stand. Next to each name, write something good about that person. If you cannot think of anything, keep trying until you do. Now pray for each of these people, giving thanks for those good traits. Resolve to do all you can to be reconciled to them.

In the days to come, as such reconciliation is achieved, scratch through the name of that person on your list. Do not be satisfied as long as a name remains.

Third Day: Read Philippians 1:5-7.

See: Paul is particularly thankful for the Philippians' "sharing in the gospel." The word that is here translated as "sharing" is *koinonia*, which has a wide variety of meanings ranging from fellowship to a corporation and including the Lord's Supper. In view of how much the Philippians had shared of their own goods with Paul, it is clear that he is thankful not only for their fellowship, but also for their spirit of sharing. That is why he declares that this has been a trait of the Philippians "from the first day until now." Remember that in Acts we were told that Lydia "prevailed" upon Paul and his companions to take lodgings in her house (Acts 16:15). Paul normally avoided receiving economic support for himself from the churches. But the Philippians were an exception "from the first day." Later on as we study this epistle we shall see why he also declares that this has continued "until now."

Paul is thankful, not only for what the Philippians are and have done, but also for what they are to become, since "the one who began a good work among you will bring it to completion by the day of Jesus Christ."

Judge: It is common to hear much talk in the church about fellowship and love, which are indeed at the center of Christianity. But if fellowship and love are only talked about, or if the talk is only a matter of feelings and does not reach into our goods and resources, such conversation soon loses its strength and becomes superficial and sentimental. As an ancient Christian writer said, "If we share in eternal goods, how are we not to share in those that perish?"

In other words, it is quite easy to declare ourselves brothers and sisters in the faith and common stockholders in a coming reign of God; but if we are not ready to share in what we now have at hand—money, time, or any other resource—it is difficult to believe that we are true brothers and sisters and partakers of the same hope.

*What signs do you see in your church of this sharing to which Paul refers?

*What signs do you see that your sharing is or is not what it ought to be?

Act: Review your expenditures during the past month. Look at your checkbook and your credit card reports. Divide a sheet in your notebook into two columns, each with a heading: (1) *On myself and my family* (2) *On others*. List your expenditures under each of the two headings. For instance, if you paid your mortgage, write that down in the first column. If you made a contribution to the church or to a charitable program, list that in the second column. Total each column. Consider whether the proportion between these two is correct and whether it reflects your Christian commitment. If you come to the conclusion that you must raise the amount in the second column, consider concrete ways to do this. Share and discuss your thoughts with your family. Pray together over it. Write down your conclusions.

Fourth Day: Read Philippians 1:8-11.

See: Paul tells the Philippians that what he is asking for them is that "your love may overflow more and more with knowledge and full insight."

Note that here "love" is not only a matter of the heart and the emotions, but also of knowledge. In order to understand fully what love is in the Bible, it is important to realize that it is not only an emotion. It is also knowledge, wisdom, and action. Only on the basis of that love can one "determine what is best" (v. 10). Without knowledge love may well determine what it should not. Therefore, Paul asks not only that the Philippians be loving, but that they will love "with knowledge and full insight." It is such love, led by knowledge and insight, that produces true sincerity "so that in the day of Christ you may be pure and blameless."

Judge: In our day in our society there is much talk of love. But by that what is often understood is an emotion, an overwhelming feeling. There is no doubt that love is indeed overwhelming and includes our emotions. But love without knowledge or insight, love that can be easily enticed by falsehood, is not necessarily a virtue.

To say that we love God, while not devoting ourselves to the knowledge of God, is to be lacking in sincerity. To say that we love our neighbors, but then not to make an effort to understand why they live as they do, is not to be truly loving. True love makes an effort to understand in order to act better—or, as Paul would say, to produce "the harvest of righteousness." For instance, if we love the needy we must understand why they are needy.

The word "love" is so often used in church that sometimes it seems to have lost its edge. What are we doing to make sure that our love includes "knowledge and insight"? When we say we love the community around the church, do we take the time to study and try to understand how that community really functions? To discover what interests rule it? To learn what its deepest problems are? Without such knowledge, our love for the community may well be no more than an ineffectual sentimentality.

Act: Try to think of something that you or your church should know so your love will be more effective. (For instance, if it is a matter of love for the community, what must you know about its functioning? If it is a matter of love toward your children, what must you know to be a better parent? If it is a matter of love for God, what studies can help you on that score?) Resolve that you will employ the three months that you will be studying these epistles to widen and deepen your knowledge of Scripture as well as of your church, your family, and yourself.

Fifth Day: Read Philippians 1:12-14.

See: Paul tells the Philippians that the evil he is suffering—his imprisonment—has resulted in good. He does not claim that God has freed him from prison, although he knows that God can do that. What he says is that his imprisonment has strengthened his witness and "the whole imperial guard" is aware of that (v.13). Although there are different interpretations of this particular phrase, many think it is an indication that Paul was imprisoned in Rome, where the imperial guard, the *praetorium*, resided.

Furthermore, Paul's imprisonment has strengthened the witness of other believers, who now "dare to speak the word with greater boldness and without fear." This is not because Paul has been freed—he has not been—but because even in his imprisonment Paul has witnessed to his faith.

Judge: Some people think, and some even preach, that when one becomes a Christian all problems are solved. We are told that believers will succeed in all they undertake; if they are ill, all they need in order to be healed is faith. In order to convince us, people who believe this will tell us of the many miracles, both in the Bible and elsewhere, by which God has responded to human need. For instance, when Peter was imprisoned, an angel came and freed him. And there is no doubt that the Bible recounts, and Christians have experienced, miracles of healing.

What these "evangelists of success" forget is that in the Bible itself God does not always solve the problems of the faithful. Paul is imprisoned, and God does not send an angel to free him.

But this does not mean that Paul has less faith than Peter. On the contrary, it appears that Paul is preaching in prison, whereas Peter was asleep when the angel came to him (Acts 12:6-7).

Act: What are your worst sufferings, the things that cause you the most anxiety, the concerns that keep you awake at night? List them in your notebook.

Now remember that the gospel does not say that these difficulties and anxieties are not important. They are very real and, since they shape our lives, they are important. What faith can do is to keep you from being overwhelmed by them and perhaps even lead you to live in them with joy and thanksgiving, following Paul's example.

Sixth Day: Read Philippians 1:15-18.

See: Paul has no illusions about why people preach the gospel. He has already told the Philippians that as a result of his testimony in prison some believers have attained new zeal in witnessing to Christ. But apparently others took Paul's imprisonment as an opportunity to undercut him, preaching and creating Christian groups that had nothing to do with Paul's work.

It would have been quite natural for Paul to be angered by the preaching of such people, a preaching that stems, not from love, but "out of selfish ambition." But Paul does not respond in anger. On the contrary, he rejoices that Christ is proclaimed "whether out of false motives or true."

Judge: Are there situations in your congregation in which issues of control seem to be more important than the mission of the church? Are there cases in which decisions are made, not on the basis of what is good or more loving, but rather on the basis of who has proposed a project, who opposes it, or who will manage the budget?

Reflect on your own attitude and actions. When someone in your congregation proposes something, do you consider first if it is a good idea or not, or do you think about who is proposing the idea and whether you like that person?

When something good does happen in your congregation, or when the community listens to its witness, do you rejoice no matter who receives the credit?

If a church of another denomination performs an outstanding service in the community or offers a strong witness, do you and your congregation rejoice as if this were of your own doing? Or do you rather try to find fault with what that other congregation is doing?

Act: Decide that from now on, when you must judge a proposal or an action, you will judge it not on the basis of who makes the proposal or takes the action, but rather on the basis of the proposal or the action itself. Make particularly sure that if the person proposing something different is someone you do not like, you will make a special effort to listen with an open mind.

Pray: "Help me, Lord, to see the work of your hands even when you perform it through hands other than mine, or even through hands that I would rather not touch. Amen."

Repeat this prayer until it really becomes the desire of your heart. Write it in your notebook and return to it as often as you find it necessary.

Seventh Day: Read Philippians 1:19-30.

See: Verse 19 implies that Paul expects to be freed through the prayers of believers and with the help of the Spirit. However, as we read on, what Paul refers to as "my deliverance" is not necessarily being freed from his chains. In the very next verse he declares that Christ will be exalted in his body, "whether by life or by death." Thus, Paul will be "delivered," no matter whether he is freed or killed. That deliverance of which he is absolutely assured does not depend on his physical freedom.

This is the context within which we must understand the oft quoted words: "For to me, living is Christ and dying is gain" (v. 21). If his jailers—or rather the empire they represent—kill him, this will be a gain for Paul. It will be a gain because even in death he will have Christ, and for him "living is Christ." Thus, Paul is speaking of a certainty not that everything will turn out rosy, but rather that, whether in life or in death, Christ will be glorified and Paul will live in Christ.

Verses 22-24 are an explanation of verse 21 and offer a glimpse of how Paul faces his imprisonment and possible death. His concern is not so much death itself or his own sufferings, but the possibility that he will not be able to continue his ministry. Were it not for that, he would be ready to die "and be with Christ." It is because his ministry is not finished that he hopes to be freed physically, as he says in verses 24 and 25. But even this is not an absolute certainty, for in verse 27 he says that what he is writing is valid "whether I come and see you or am absent and hear about you."

Verses 27 and following tell us what Paul hopes for himself and for the Philippians. His great hope is not necessarily that an angel will come and open the doors of his prison, even though one may surmise that he knows the story of how Peter was freed in similar circumstances and will certainly remember his own experience of being freed in Philippi itself. Paul's great hope is that the Philippians will live "in a manner worthy of the gospel of Christ." He does not expect that they will be free of problems and conflicts, but hopes that in their struggles they will remain "firm in one spirit ... in no way intimidated by your opponents." In short, Paul hopes that his experience of having Christians speak fearlessly because they have seen his own attitude in prison will be also the experience of the Philippians.

Finally, the passage closes with words that merit serious consideration. Just as in Paul's life faith and suffering are joined, so must they be joined in the life of the Philippians. Paul speaks of his own "struggle" in two ways, referring to what the Philippians have *seen* and what they now *hear*. What they have seen is Paul's ministry in Philippi, as described in Acts 16:11-40. What they now hear is word of Paul's imprisonment.

Judge: This passage becomes particularly interesting if we read it keeping in mind what Acts tells us about Paul's ministry in

Philippi. It was precisely in Philippi that Paul was in prison and God's power was made manifest in an earthquake that resulted in Paul's liberation and the conversion of the jailer. One can imagine how often that story must have been told in Philippi. Now, upon hearing that once again he is a prisoner, they will be expecting that he will be freed again. Perhaps an earthquake will open the gates of his prison. Or perhaps an angel will come and free him as in the case of Peter.

While writing to the Philippians from prison, Paul would be remembering that night in the jail in Philippi when he and Silas sang hymns and the Lord intervened. He would also know that the Philippians, upon receiving his letter from prison, would also remember those events and probably expect a similar miracle.

There are two alternatives open to Paul in prison. The first would be most common and normal: he could lose heart and begin doubting his own ministry. That is what many of us tend to do when something does not turn out the way we hoped. His other option would be to think that, since he has faith and since the Lord has freed him once, he will necessarily be freed a second time. Many Christians imagine that this is the nature of faith and that those who are not certain that God will free them from some difficulty or heal them from a disease are simply lacking in faith.

But Paul does not follow either of these options. He does not lose heart, because he knows that the Lord in whom he has believed and who freed him from his chains in Philippi is more powerful than any chain or empire. Nor does he take for granted that God will repeat the miracle and free him from jail once again. What he does is simply put both his life and his death in the hands of the Lord of life and death. This is what allows him to rejoice even while in prison. But there is more. Paul puts forth his own struggles as a sign of what will be true also for the Philippians. It is not only Christ who triumphed through his sufferings on the cross, or Paul who now triumphs in his prison. All Christians have the same calling. And this is not a curse, for Paul tells the Philippians that God "has graciously granted you the privilege not only of believing in Christ, but of suffering for him as well" (v. 29).

Act: Think of a personal difficulty that you are going though. (For instance, an illness, a financial bind, or a family problem.) Write in your notebook: "No matter whether _____ or _____ Christ will be exalted in me, for to me living is Christ and dying is gain."

Now fill the blanks with whatever is appropriate in your case. (For instance, "I am healed or not," or "I find a job or am unemployed.") Read over what you have written several times. If you are alone, read it out loud. Pray that what you have written will become a reality in your life.

For Group Study

Before the group meets, ask some of the members to read the story of Paul's sojourn in Philippi (Acts 16). When the group gathers, these people will play the role of Philippian Christians who remember all of this and have just received Paul's letter.

In the group session, read the passage from the epistle out loud, a few words at a time, and ask these "Philippians" to comment. Each member of the group should do what is suggested above under the heading **Act**. Suggest that each one think about the matter and write what is directed there. If the members of the group have a level of trust that allows for it, this would be a good opportunity for them to share their concerns and to discuss and comment on how this Scripture helps them face such concerns.

W E E K
TWO

First Day: Read Philippians 2:1-2.

See: Verse 1 is entirely in the subjunctive mood: "*If* then there is any encouragement in Christ, any consolation from love, any sharing in the Spirit, any compassion and sympathy...." Naturally, Paul does believe that such things exist, and therefo re what follows in verse 2 is to be taken as certain. If your friends say, for instance, "If the sun rises tomorrow, we'll come see you," this means that they will in fact go. Likewise, when Paul says, "If there is," referring to things that are absolutely certain, he is also affirming what follows.

Verse 2 shows how important unity among believers is for Paul. What will make his joy complete is precisely that unity. Note that Paul describes that unity in three ways: being "of the same mind, having the same love, being in full accord."

Judge: Here we find again the word "joy." But now we are told that what will make joy complete is unity among the Philippians. Have you experienced this joy of unity in your own family? When there are tensions and misunderstandings, can people be truly joyous? In order for each member of the family to have joy, the entire family must be reconciled, love one another, stop quarreling.

The same is true of the church. The church is supposed to be a joyful place. We express that joy in our songs of praise and our prayers of thanksgiving. But the fact is that such joy cannot be "complete"—as Paul says—if there is among us jealousy, quarreling, and ill will. Our joy comes from the Lord but is only made complete in our love for one another. Without such love, joy is incomplete. This is why throughout the entire epistle Paul will insist on unity, and this is also why in these verses he tells the Philippians that they are to be united in three ways: being of the same mind, having the same love, and being in full accord.

Is this the way your congregation lives? If not, what can you do to promote unity?

Is there any chance that you may be contributing to division and resentment?

Act: Think of someone in the congregation who has offended you or from whom you have grown distant for whatever reason. Resolve to make every effort to come close to this person. If it is possible, stop your Bible study right now and make a phone call to that person. Only do pray before you call, and pray again afterward. Write down your reflections as well as any thoughts about future steps.

Second Day: Read Philippians 2:3-4.

See: In these two verses Paul points to the source of divisions within the church: doing things "from selfish ambition or conceit" and looking "to your own interests." In other words, while the two verses studied yesterday presented unity, these two verses are about division. Paul lists three motivations that create division: first, doing things "from selfish ambition"; second, doing them out of "conceit"; third, looking "to your own interests."

Judge: Consider these three motivators, and ask yourself if you have ever been guilty of any of them. For instance, we act from "selfish ambition" when someone proposes that the church take an action and we oppose the suggestion, not because the idea is not a good one, but simply because it was not our idea. Our opposition often leads to division, for most probably that other person will respond in kind when the opportunity arises. Eventually we will have two separate groups, each opposing the other without even knowing why.

We are acting out of "conceit" when we volunteer for a task, not because the task is important but so our devotion may be recognized. Many congregations suffer division because in listing the services of some members, the pastor neglects to mention others. If we do things out of conceit it is difficult for us if our work is overlooked. If someone else is recognized but we aren't, jealousy arises. Eventually the congregation may have to spend all the time making certain that each member receives the exact measure of recognition he or she deserves. Since this is impossible, the result will be ill will and resentment.

Finally, unity suffers when we look after our "own interests." In any community there are always conflicting interests. They may appear in the simplest of matters. Suppose we are discussing when a committee of three is to meet. Wednesday is not convenient for me; Elizabeth would rather not meet on Thursday; but Joe can only meet on Wednesday or Thursday. In such a case, if I insist on not meeting on Wednesday and Elizabeth remains adamant about Thursday, we shall never meet. If I insist on meeting on Thursday, even though Elizabeth's reasons are weightier than mine and meeting on Wednesday would cause serious difficulty for her, I shall be doing a disservice to the unity of the church and the work of the committee.

Act: Write down in a column, one above the other: *ambition, conceit, self-interest.* Review the decisions that have been made during the past month or so within your family or within your congregation, and review your role in these decisions. Ask yourself if any of the three things you have listed describe some of the reasons for what you said or did. If you find any, make a note next to that word. Pray, asking forgiveness for the past and guidance for the future. Consider if there are any ways in which you may undo any harm that has been done. If you can think of nothing to write next to those words, pray, asking God to free you from these three temptations and to make you think twice when they are present.

Third Day: Read Philippians 2:5-11.

See: This passage is of such importance that we shall devote three days to it. Read the entire passage, although today and tomorrow we shall be dealing mostly with verses 5-8 and the day after tomorrow with verses 9-11.

Verse 5 is the heart of the passage, for it relates the attitude that Christians ought to have with that of Jesus. The mind that should be in us is the same that was in him. That we are to be humble and to esteem others above ourselves is not a mere piece of wise counsel, but is based on the example of Jesus.

Verses 6-11 are a hymn. It is difficult to see this in translation, but in the Greek original it is clear that this is poetry. No one knows whether Paul composed this hymn as part of his letter or simply quoted one that was already circulating among Christians—as is the case, for instance, when in order to remind someone that they may be wrong we quote "I once was blind but now I see." In any case, here we have the words of one of the most ancient Christian hymns.

The theme of the hymn is obvious: the Lord's initial glory, his willingness to empty himself of that glory, to make himself obedient, and finally, his glorification. Christ was ready to empty himself of his glory and to become as a servant—or as a slave, for in Greek the two words are the same.

When the hymn refers to the death of Jesus, "even death on a cross," the emphasis is not on suffering but on humiliation. Crucifixion was reserved for the worst criminals and for those of the lower classes. Among Jews, to be "hung from a tree" was a sign of being accursed (Galatians 3:13). What is being underscored here is Jesus' humility, which led him to a death that religious people would see as a sign that God had abandoned him.

Judge: Why do you think Paul placed this hymn in the letter? Do you see the relationship between the hymn and what Paul has been saying in the verses we have been studying? Not doing things out of conceit, ambition, or self-interest is grounded on having "the same mind that was in Christ Jesus." Jesus did these things not out of ambition or conceit, but out of love and obedience. That love and obedience led him to a profound humility that is to serve as example and source for all Christian humility. It is common to hear in church that we ought to "have Jesus in our heart," or that we are to "love Jesus." Do you think that it is possible to love Jesus and still act only out of ambition, conceit, or self-interest? What do you understand by having the mind that was in Christ Jesus?

Act: Remember the hymn "Thou didst leave Thy throne and Thy kingly crown," particularly the refrain: "O come to my heart, Lord Jesus: there is room in my heart for Thee!" Turn those words into your prayer. In inviting Jesus to come into your heart, ask him also to give you the mind that was in him which freed him from ambition and conceit, making him obedient to the point of death on a cross.

Think of whatever stands in the way of your doing what Paul asks of the Philippians, that they be of the same mind, that they do nothing out of conceit or ambition or self-interest. Every time you think of such an obstacle to your obedience, write in your notebook: "Come into my heart, Lord Jesus. Free me from _____."

Write as many such phrases as you find necessary. Once you have finished your list, read it out loud in prayer two or three times.

Fourth Day: Read Philippians 2:5-11.

See: As we saw yesterday, we shall devote three days to the study of this hymn, which is the heart of the epistle. Yesterday we studied as far as verse 8, and today we shall return to the same section in order to look at verses 9-11 tomorrow. Therefore, begin your study by reading the entire passage once again.

Judge: Nothing is more harmful to Christian witness than divisions, ill will, and gossip. Unfortunately, such things are quite common among Christians. Someone gets upset because he worked hard at preparing a program and was not thanked for it. Another feels offended by something the pastor said. A third insists that things be done as she says, and if they are done otherwise she will not cooperate. Meanwhile, gossip runs amok: Some talk behind the backs of others, perhaps hoping that by putting others down they will appear as better Christians. Others listen to them, perhaps because when they are told of the sins and shortcomings of the rest they will feel less guilty about their own. As a result, the community of believers is divided and our witness is weakened, for those who see us have reason to wonder if the gospel really has the power to redeem and to change people.

Paul knows that this is a danger for any human group, particularly for the church. He also knows where the root of this evil lies: in inordinate pride. All want to draw attention to themselves and be told how important they are.

In order to attack the root of this evil, Paul offers the Philippians—and offers us today—the example of Jesus Christ. Who more than he had something to boast about? Who more than he had the right to be served? Yet, rather than insisting on his glory, and rather than demanding service from others, he emptied himself of his glory and became one of us. And while he was among us he made it quite clear that he came not to be served but to serve.

If there are divisions, ill will, and gossip among us, this is a sign that we do not have "the mind that was in Christ Jesus." Those who claim to be holier, yet who speak ill of those who are less, are not as holy as they claim. Those who claim to be most faithful and hardworking and ready to serve in any capacity as long as they are properly thanked and acknowledged from the pulpit are not as faithful as they claim.

Act: How are divisions healed in the church? Certainly not by blaming one another or by saying, "You started it." Nor are they healed by getting rid of those who are in disagreement with the leadership. They are healed by sharing the mind that was in

Jesus Christ, a mind of humility and service. They are healed when we follow Paul's advice: "In humility regard others as better than yourselves" (2:3).

During the coming week, whenever you are tempted to believe that you are better than someone else, or that you have worked harder than the rest, or that your work has not been duly acknowledged, remember "the mind that was in Christ Jesus."

Fifth Day: Read Philippians 2:5-11.

See: The hymn ends with the glorification of Jesus, whom God "highly exalted." Read the hymn again, but now look particularly at verses 9-11. Note that Jesus is completely glorified. Note particularly how often the word "every" appears: every name, every knee, every tongue. What this means is that nothing is outside the scope and power of Jesus. He who humbled himself unto death, even death on a cross, now has such power and such glory that his name is above *every* name, *every* knee bends before him, and *every* tongue confesses that he is Lord. Nothing is excluded. Nothing is beyond the reach of the power of Christ Jesus.

If some rebel and refuse to accept him, they are simply rejecting what is indeed a fact. If there are still areas of political, economic, and social life, as well as areas in our own lives, that are not subject to his lordship, Paul knows and proclaims that in the end all of these things will be subject to him, when "at the name of Jesus every knee should bend, in heaven and on earth and under the earth, and every tongue should confess that Jesus Christ is Lord, to the glory of God the Father."

Judge: In the first part of the hymn Paul dwells on the suffering, obedience, and humility of Jesus. Now he turns to what seems the exact opposite, the universal lordship of Jesus.

Why do you think this expectation of the absolute and universal lordship of Jesus is important? In order to respond to that question, imagine the opposite. Imagine Paul believing that Jesus is Lord only over some things and not others. Imagine, for instance, that Paul does not believe that Jesus is Lord above the empire in whose prisons he now is. Imagine Paul believing that the last word belongs to the Roman Empire. In that case, would he be able to remain joyful even while he is in prison?

Is the same not true of other believers? Could it be that when we lack in joy we are really lacking in faith? Could it be that we have little strength in the midst of difficulties because we do not believe that the last word belongs to Jesus?

Act: Think about what scares you more than anything else—death, disease, unemployment. Remember the words of Jesus: "All authority in heaven and on earth has been given to me" (Matthew 28:18). Now pray as follows:

"Lord, you know that I am afraid of _____. But even over that you are Lord. Grant me the faith I need to trust you and thus to rejoice and serve you in all things."

Repeat this prayer or one like it whenever fear threatens your joy.

Sixth Day: Read Philippians 2:12-18.

See: Note that the passage begins with the theme of obedience, and remember that in the hymn we have just studied, Paul underlines how Jesus "became obedient to the point of death." Thus, Paul is still referring to that hymn and presenting Jesus as the example to be followed—an example of obedience. It is as a result of that example that all things are to be done "without murmuring and arguing."

When things are done in that spirit, Paul declares that Christians are "blameless and innocent, children of God without blemish." The result is that such people "shine like stars in the world." On the basis of the Philippians' obedience, Paul is able to "boast on the day of Christ," that is, the day on which Christ will show forth his power, as is announced in the hymn that we have just studied. Furthermore, the power of this conviction is such that Paul will be able to be glad and rejoice even if he is killed ("if I am being poured out as a libation over the sacrifice and the offering of your faith").

The passage ends with beautiful words on Christian joy: Paul rejoices with the Philippians, and they in turn are to rejoice with him.

Judge: Although this passage is not as well known as the hymn that precedes it, here we find once again the central themes of the epistle: obedience, joy, and the need to avoid "murmuring and arguing."

However, the theme of presence and absence is also important here. Paul tells his readers that they are to be just as obedient in his absence as they are in his presence. Danish theologian Søren Kierkegaard pointed out that a soldier's obedience is shown not as much when the captain is present as when he is absent. Paul calls the Philippians to be obedient in his absence.

But in verse 16, when referring to "the day of Christ," Paul implies that there is a sense in which Christ too is absent—that is, that his presence is not yet shown with the power that it will have in the end. Thus, Paul himself obeys Christ who is not fully present and manifest, and calls on the Philippians to do the same.

Join this with what Paul has said before regarding mutual rejoicing between himself and the Philippians. What all of this means is that even though Christ is not yet manifest in all his glory and power, Paul, the Philippians, and anyone else who believes in Christ can now rejoice, for "the day of Christ" is coming. And we can also obey Christ even though his power is not yet fully manifested.

Act: Are you and your church "like stars in the world"? Note that in order for this to be so, believers must mutually rejoice in the faith and victories of one another. When was the last time you approached someone in your church to express words of encouragement, indicating that their presence and their contribution to the life of the church was a cause of joy for you?

Resolve each day to approach someone and tell him or her that you rejoice in their presence and their contribution to the life of the community. In order to do this sincerely, you will need to take the time to think about various people and the gifts they bring. Make a particular effort to achieve a sincere joy in those people who seem to be marginal to the life of the congregation. For instance, it is easy to tell the pastor or the treasurer that their work is important. It is more difficult to rejoice in the presence of others who draw less attention to themselves.

Pray for these people and for yourself, so that God will lead you to rejoice in their presence. Go and talk to them. Or, as Paul would say, rejoice with them and invite them to rejoice with you.

Seventh Day: Read Philippians 2:19-30.

See: This passage revolves around two of Paul's companions: Timothy (verses 19-24) and Epaphroditus (verses 25-30).

Much more is known about Timothy than about Epaphroditus. We have already seen that Paul himself says that he is writing this letter jointly with Timothy (1:1). According to Acts, Timothy was from Lystra, having a pagan father and a mother who was a believer, Eunice. He himself became a leader among believers in Lystra and Iconium, and it was there that Paul met him.

When Paul and Barnabas parted company and Paul undertook his second missionary journey, he was accompanied by Timothy instead of John Mark, who had abandoned him during the first journey. Since it was widely known that Timothy's father was a pagan but he himself was considered a Jew because his mother was Jewish, Paul had him circumcised in order to avoid scandal among the Jews they would meet.

Apparently, although Timothy remained with Paul during most of his journeys, the two parted several times, particularly when it was necessary to send Timothy to another city. Thus, for instance, in 1 Thessalonians 3:1-5, we learn that Paul sent Timothy to Thessalonica so that he would confirm the believers in that town. Here we see that the same is about to take place. Paul intends to send Timothy to Philippi as soon as he has something to tell the Philippians regarding the outcome of his own imprisonment ("as soon as I see how things go with me").

Apparently Paul's plan to send Timothy to Philippi has a double purpose. First, Timothy is to let the Philippians know the outcome of Paul's imprisonment. Second, he is to return to Paul bringing trustworthy news of the church in Philippi.

Epaphroditus is less known. This name, which was then fairly common, appears only here in the New Testament. But in Philemon and Colossians, Paul refers to "Epaphras," which is an abbreviation of the same name. They are possibly the same person, although the distance between Philippi and Colossae would suggest otherwise. At any rate, Epaphroditus was sent to Paul by the Philippians (see 4:18), carrying a contribution to Paul's mission. After meeting with Paul, he became gravely ill, to the point that there was fear for his life. But now Epaphroditus is better, and he is concerned that his mother church in Philippi may have heard of his illness but not of his improvement. Therefore Paul decides to send him back to Philippi. It is even likely that the occasion for the entire letter may have been Epaphroditus's return to Philippi.

Judge: Up to this point Paul has been discussing joy and Christian unity in general terms, grounding them on the example of Jesus and calling his readers to follow that example, so that there may be unity among them. Now, in what would seem to be an interruption, he leaves aside that discussion of general themes in order to speak of two specific companions, Timothy and Epaphroditus. One of them has been Paul's companion for quite some time. The other has reached Paul more recently, apparently bringing a gift or contribution from his own church in Philippi. Is this really an interruption in Paul's line of thought? Or is it rather a specific illustration of what Paul has been saying from the very beginning of his letter? Is it not the case that the joy and unity that Paul so commends exists only in concrete cases, when we practice them with specific people?

Think about this for a few minutes. It is fairly easy to love humankind in general. But Jesus commanded us to love our neighbor, that particular example of humankind who is among us. This is much more difficult. We are never bothered or asked to do anything by "humankind" in general. Those who require our service, support, and help are specific people whom we encounter in the paths of life. It is quite easy to rejoice in the church universal. It is more difficult to rejoice in the local congregation, where we know one another and our foibles and defects.

Therefore, in mentioning Timothy and Epaphroditus, Paul is reminding us, even though indirectly, that love and joy have to be directed toward specific people; that we cannot claim that we love humankind while we look down on the sister or the brother who sits in a pew near us.

Act: The church in Philippi heard Paul was in prison and in need, and sent help to him. Try to have your church ask who are needy, both among its members and in the neighborhood, and what the church can do for them. This could be physical help, such as food, clothing, or employment. It could also be spiritual and emotional help, such as visiting someone who is ill or in prison. However, do not wait until your congregation as a whole undertakes this task. Begin doing it yourself. Resolve that during the coming week you will visit someone who is in need.

If your congregation publishes a directory, or if there is a list of members available to you, try to find there the names of three or four people you do not know. Write their names in your notebook and set out to know them better. (It is difficult to respond to the needs of people without knowing them and thus knowing what they need.) Begin by praying for the people on your list.

For Group Study

Write the name of each of the participants in the group on a slip of paper. Distribute these papers among the group. Ask each person to imagine that he or she is Paul writing a letter to another church and recommending the person whose name they have. What would the letter say? If any wish to respond to this question out loud, allow them to do so. By doing this, we cement our relationship and it is easier for us to rejoice in our unity and love, as Paul does with the Philippians.

WEEK

THREE

First Day: Read Philippians 3:1.

See: In this verse Paul returns to the central theme of the epistle: joy. Even so, we have not yet come to the place in the letter where Paul most underscores joy. After two weeks studying this letter, and dealing with the subject of joy over and over, it may look as if Paul is repeating himself and it is time to move on to something else.

On this score, it is interesting to note that Paul knows he is repeating himself. That is why he says, "To write the same things to you is not troublesome to me." In other words, no matter how often he has said it, he would repeat it again as many times as necessary. He also tells his readers that he does this for their own good, because repeating himself is "a safeguard" for them.

Referring to his insistence on joy as a safeguard, Paul indicates that joy is central for Christian faith and obedience. Without joy, even in the midst of difficulties, one is not truly a believer in Jesus Christ and his victory. Therefore, it is good for the Philippians to hear once again about joy, for this strengthens them in their faith.

Judge: Perhaps the Philippians felt that Paul was beating the subject of joy into the ground. After two weeks writing and commenting on it, I certainly feel that way. You probably agree. Isn't it high time to move to something else?

Why do you think Paul is so insistent on the subject of joy? Personally, I must confess that even though I may feel I have heard enough about this, I still need more. Even though for two weeks I have been reflecting and writing on this subject, when I make an inventory of my own life and feelings during those two weeks I discover that I have not always felt or shown that joy of which Paul speaks. More than once, facing one of the many small aggravations of daily life, I have set joy aside and have come very close to doubt and discouragement. When a few days ago I did not feel well, and when a brother in the faith let me down, I easily set aside all that I had thought and written about joy.

Could the same be the case with you? Although it may be difficult to accept, is it possible that you also need to hear more about joy?

Act: Review the two weeks you have just completed. Have you really been flooded by that joy of which Paul speaks? Have there been circumstances or moments in which you have allowed yourself to be carried away by discouragement or bitterness? Have you shown a joy greater and deeper than the "happiness" of people when all goes well?

Write down some of the cases in which you left Christian joy aside. Reflect on each of them. Think of what you could or should have done or thought in each of those cases. Write down your reflections. End your study period with a prayer, asking God to help you feel and show a deep Christian joy in all circumstances of your life.

Second Day: Read Philippians 3:2-3.

See: It is shocking, immediately after all Paul has said, to find him referring to other people as "dogs." But we must remind ourselves that Christian joy is not based on illusions about the goodness of life, of the world, or of other people. On the contrary, Christian joy, precisely because it makes us truly free, allows us to look on all these with realism.

In this case, Paul takes an epithet that some of the more fanatical Jews applied to the Gentiles, whom they called "dogs," and applies it to what he would call judaizing Christians who undermine the joy of the Philippians.

Apparently, the "dogs," the "evil workers," and "those who mutilate the flesh" are the same. The second of these phrases is probably a reference to the Lord's vineyard and to workers who do not do their master's will. The last is probably a reference to those who insist on physical circumcision.

It is not certain that these "judaizers" were in fact Jews. Indeed, it is quite likely that they were Gentile converts to Christianity, who, eager not to be less than the rest, insisted on the need for all Christians, Jewish as well as Gentile, to be circumcised and to keep the Law. Against such claims, Paul declares that "it is we who are the circumcision" (that is, the People of God), and that what characterizes us is that we "worship in the Spirit of God," and "have no confidence in the flesh."

Paul intentionally uses this phrase with two meanings. On the one hand, we have "no confidence in the flesh" in the sense that our faith does not rest in the physical act of circumcision. On the other hand, we have "no confidence in the flesh" in the sense that our faith rests not in any creature, not even in our own actions, but in the action of God in Jesus Christ.

Judge: Why do you think Paul calls his opponents by such a harsh epithet as "dogs"? Did he always speak so harshly of those who opposed him? (Think about his other epistles, and you will not find many cases in which Paul uses such harsh words to refer to anybody.) Did he simply lose patience with these people? Or is it rather that in this particular case he was convinced that these people's teachings threatened the very heart of the Christian faith?

Do you ever speak so harshly of others? In such a case, are your words justified because what is at stake is of supreme importance? Or are your words simply a way to vent your anger and frustration? If the latter, remember that the tongue, even though a small organ, can do great damage (James 3:5). On the other hand, when hard words are necessary, are you ready to speak them, or do you rather allow yourself to be led by your desire to avoid conflict, even when what is at stake is of vital importance? How do you decide when to speak harshly, when to speak softly, and when to remain silent?

Act: After reflecting on the above questions, pray: "Lord, take not only my life, but also my words, so that the sayings of my mouth may be acceptable to you. When it is time to speak a harsh word of judgment and correction, give me the courage and wisdom to do so. When what is needed is a soft word of support and compassion, give me the wisdom to provide such a word. And when what is needful is to say nothing, give me the gift of silence. I pray in the name of Jesus Christ, your Word who spoke in the beginning, your Word who remained silent before Pilate, your Word who will have the last word. Amen."

Third Day: Read Philippians 3:4-6.

See: In order to refute the "dogs" who claim that what is important is to be circumcised and obey the Law, Paul tells the Philippians that he could boast about that and much more. If it were a matter of being "confident in the flesh," no one would have more right to such confidence than Paul himself. Paul has not only been circumcised, but he received the rite on the eighth day after his birth because he was born "a member of the People of Israel." If, as is likely, Paul's opponents were not Jewish by birth, what Paul is saying is that he is not a make-believe Jew like they, but a true Jew from his very birth. His circumcision was not a matter of someone convincing him, but was rather the custom of his people for many centuries.

Paul is "of the tribe of Benjamin." Quite possibly this is why his name was Saul, the name of the only King of Israel out of the tribe of Benjamin. And not only that, but Paul is "a Hebrew born of Hebrews" and was brought up as a Pharisee, that is, as a person convinced that it was necessary to obey the Law in all particulars.

And if it is a matter of religious zeal, here too Paul exceeds these latter-day Jews, for it was because of such zeal that he had persecuted the church. Thus, as regards the righteousness that is by the Law and which the "dogs" now proclaim, Paul was always "blameless."

Judge: Why do you think that Paul now speaks of himself, of his origins and religious zeal? Is it in order to boast or is it rather to show that no one has anything to boast about? Tomorrow we shall see that Paul can speak very negatively about all these things. Therefore, what Paul intends with these verses is not to boast about himself but rather to prevent all boasting.

What do you boast about? What aspects of your life are you most proud of? Your economic achievements? Your friends and connections? Your studies? Your authority in the church, at work, or in the neighborhood? Your religious life and holiness? Your faithfulness in pursuing these three months of study? Each of these things may be very good, but if the day comes when you trust in any of them as the source of your joy and salvation, you have fallen into the same trap as those whom Paul refuted because they trusted in the flesh and in circumcision.

Why do you think Paul writes these words in the very middle of a letter about joy? Is it not because when one trusts in such things one loses the true Christian joy? Think about it. If we trust something we do or something we have, we are always at risk of losing it. As long as we fear that risk, as long as our ultimate trust is not in God, we shall not have that deep joy that is an essential element of the Christian life. If, however, our salvation and our future do not depend on us, but are always in the hands of God, and if we know that God loves us, then nothing nor anyone will be able to take that joy from us, because nothing will be able to take Christ's love away from us.

Act: Make a list of all the things of which you could boast. Next to each write: "Thank you, Lord." Take the time to think about what you are writing until you see that if you have anything to boast about this is because God has given it to you. If there is something about which you cannot simply say, "Thank you, Lord," beware! This may be a sign of danger. Whatever it is, perhaps it is not as good as you would like to think. If you find it difficult to say, "Thank you, Lord," consider the possibility of saying, "Take it away from me, Lord." If you feel it is best to write these latter words, do so.

Fourth Day: Read Philippians 3:7-9.

See: Paul has much to boast about. But all that is quite useless. All those things of which he used to be proud are now "loss" and "rubbish." Why? Because they lead to inordinate pride, trusting in the "flesh," and therefore to setting aside the grace of Christ.

Note that the reason Paul now declares all his achievements to be "rubbish," and is quite willing to lose them all, is in order to "gain Christ and be found in him." There is a contrast here between losing all and being "found" in Christ. In a way, one is the counterpart of the other: without being ready to lose all it is not possible to be found in Christ.

Finally, in verse 9 there is a contrast between two sorts of righteousness. The first is one's own righteousness based on obedience to the Law. That is the righteousness that the "dogs" insist the Philippians need: they will be righteous if they are circumcised and keep the Law. The second sort of righteousness is not something one achieves or attains but rather "one that comes through faith in Christ." One righteousness is Paul's own; the second is "from God." It is never ours in the sense that we own it or may deserve it. It is from God and forever remains God's.

Judge: Most of us have not been raised as Jews and therefore the matter of the Law does not touch us in the same way it did Paul and his contemporaries. But we do have other things in which we trust instead of Christ.

One of these things is all that we have done in the past, and especially what we have done in matters of religion. We like to boast that we have attended church for twenty, thirty, or forty years. Particularly those of us who are older rejoice in the things we did in the past, the programs we organized, the converts we brought to the church.

We also like to boast about our present religious life. We are proud that we are not dissolute like so many around us. We boast of being faithful Christians, attending church regularly, and supporting all its programs.

Paul, however, tells us that what may at first may seem "gain" is actually "loss" and "rubbish." This is particularly true of those things which society at large considers signs of success in life: money, good employment, prestige, power. Harsh as it may seem, to trust in such things is not to be faithful to Christ Jesus.

Something similar may be said about those things that we religious people consider signs of faith: church attendance, offering, purity of life. All of these are good as long as they are not a substitute for faith in Christ Jesus. To trust in such things is not to trust our Lord. Thus good things, when they become a substitute for faith in Christ, are only a burden in the race toward the goal of the Christian life. What Christ wants is for us to trust him, and out of such trust faithfulness will flow. Our trust is to be not in our own faithfulness or goodness, but in Christ. He is the beginning as well as the goal of Christian life.

Act: Since what we have to learn is how to trust God and not ourselves, on this occasion limit your action to praying: "Lord, I have believed in you and you have given me eternal life. Help me trust you, and only you, so that you may be my gain and my goal. For your sake, and for the sake of being found in you, help me consider all else as loss and rubbish. Amen."

Fifth Day: Read Philippians 3:10-11.

See: Paul's purpose in being ready to lose all in order to be found in Christ is to know him "and the power of his resurrection." However, this comes only when one experiences "the sharing of his sufferings by becoming like him in his death." To know Christ is to share in his resurrection and also in his sufferings and his death. The implication is that without sharing in suffering and death it is not possible to share in resurrection.

Judge: What might be the meaning today of sharing in the sufferings and death of Jesus? Although even today in other parts of the world there are Christians who suffer physical persecution, sometimes unto death, by and large our situation is quite different. Perhaps someone may mock us because of our faith, or hinder us from advancement in work or in study; but that is minor compared to the sufferings of Christ, of Paul, or of the Philippians. To claim that if somebody mocks us we are sharing in the sufferings of Christ is, at the very least, a gross exaggeration. Therefore, we have to ask once again: What is the meaning today of sharing in the sufferings and death of Jesus?

Think about that question and consider the following answer: Although it is quite true that we are very seldom persecuted as believers it is also true that even today there are vast numbers of people who suffer. There are abandoned children, hungry people, homeless people. There are millions who are undernourished, uprooted from their own lands, humiliated and broken by human injustice or by disease. In such a world, if we are to share in the sufferings of Christ, we are to do it by means of solidarity with those who suffer, suffering with them. Jesus has told us that if we give drink, food, or shelter to someone needing them, we do it to him. Thus if we suffer for the sake of someone who is needy or oppressed, because we demand justice or food for them, perhaps this is a way to begin suffering with Jesus.

Our own comfort and leisure encourage us to ignore such people. But if we allow ourselves to be driven by such inclinations, we shall not be sharing in the sufferings of Christ, and therefore we shall also not be sharing in his resurrection.

Act: Think of someone you know who is suffering. Ask yourself how you can alleviate that suffering, how you may take upon yourself some of that person's burden. For instance, if you are thinking of hungry children in a faraway land, you may refrain from buying something you really wish to have and send your money to a program that will feed those children. Or, if it is a person in your church who is suffering from a painful illness, you can turn off your TV and go visit that person to find out if there is anything that you can do to alleviate his or her pain and loneliness.

Write down what you have decided to do. In a few days, read once again what you wrote. Did you actually do it? Are you rejoicing because you did it? Could this be part of what Paul means when he speaks of the relationship between joy and Christian faith?

Sixth Day: Read Philippians 3:12-14.

See: Paul now turns to the metaphor of an athlete running a race. Races were one of the favorite sports of the time. This is why there are in Paul's epistles, as well as in other books of the New Testament, several references to athletes training to run and to others who attain the crown of victory—much as today preachers may use illustrations taken from baseball.

In this case, Paul speaks of obtaining or grasping something. This may refer to races in which the goal was to grasp a ring or some other prize. Paul's main point is that he is running in order to reach the goal.

But the text complicates matters, for Paul speaks of making something his own "because Christ Jesus has made me his own." In other words, the one who has grasped him and placed him in the race will lead him to the goal. Once again, righteousness is not a goal that Paul can reach on his own; it is Christ who has grasped Paul, and therefore Paul seeks to grasp the goal of his life. This is why Paul joyfully trusts in reaching the goal.

Even so, the image of Christian life as a race is very helpful. Paul, even though he is an apostle, does not claim to have reached the goal but rather declares that "forgetting what lies behind and straining forward to what lies ahead, I press on toward the goal."

Judge: We often hear that Christian life is only a matter of "being born again." There is no doubt that to be a true follower of Jesus Christ one has to be born of the Spirit. There has to be a turning around in which the old life of sin is left behind and the new life begins. But that is only the beginning. After that comes the "race," an entire process of discipline and obedience. This is what some call "sanctification."

Why do you think this race, this discipline of sanctification, receives so little attention? It is true that when dealing with sanctification we must be careful lest we fall into the trap of self-righteousness, of thinking that we are saved through our holiness or our religiosity or our disciplined life. Still, it is important to remember that true discipleship leads to acting as Christ did, offering our lives for others, proclaiming and demanding justice, giving signs of love.

Act: The very fact that you have set aside time for this discipline of Bible study shows that you are interested in growing in your faith and obedience. You wish to move forward in the race of Christian life. But it is important to remember that such a discipline is not merely a matter of study and reflection; it is also a matter of obedience, of Christ making us his own.

Review your "Christian race." Remember the times of great faith, joy, and enthusiasm. Remember also the falls, doubts, and dark times. Ask God to help you during your race and to run along with you, as if God had you by the hand, pulling you along, so that you may run because Christ has made you his own.

Seventh Day: Read Philippians 3:15-21.

See: It may be surprising to see Paul referring to himself as "mature" just after he has declared that he has not yet obtained the goal. These words would be even more surprising if the text were translated differently, for the word that our Bible translates as "mature" is literally "perfect." This is because the very word "perfect" has two distinct but parallel meanings. In one sense, perfection comes only at the end of the race. In another, it lies in being properly equipped to run the race, in having healthy legs and feet. Thus, Paul is referring here not to a small group of special believers who are "mature" in the sense that they have reached the goal, but rather to those who are true athletes ready for the race.

These people are to be "of the same mind." We have encountered this theme of unity and harmony several times before, and we shall deal with it next week. This is a central theme for Paul, who is concerned that divisions among believers may rob them of joy and weaken their witness. Furthermore, this unity is so important that if anyone disrupts it, God will reveal the disruption.

Verse 17 suggests one of the best ways to secure unity: imitating the best examples of Christian life in the community. Here Paul invites the Philippians to imitate him and others "who live according to the example you have in us." Verse 18 is the heart of this passage. Paul is warning his readers against certain people who "live as enemies of the cross of Christ." In the next verse he describes them in four bold strokes: (1) their end is destruction; (2) their god is their belly; (3) their glory is in their shame; (4) their minds are set on earthly things.

In contrast to such people, true believers know that "our citizenship is in heaven." True believers hope in the Lord, who comes from heaven—and not in something that is earthly or serves their own belly, as do the enemies of the cross. The Savior will transform believers radically, so that "the body of our humiliation" will be "conformed to the body of his glory." And if anyone wonders how this Savior will do such a thing, Paul responds that he will do it with his own sustaining and creating power, "the power that also enables him to make all things subject to himself."

Judge: Much could be said about this passage, but let us focus on the contrast at the very heart of the text: the "enemies of the cross of Christ" on the one hand, and those "whose citizenship is in heaven" on the other.

In a way, Paul is reiterating what he has indicated earlier in the epistle: the sharp contrast between two ways of looking at things, or between two ways of living. It is because of this contrast that Paul has earlier declared that what was once to him gain he now considers loss or rubbish.

Think about this contrast. What is the meaning of being an enemy of the cross of Christ? What makes one a friend of the cross of Christ? Does it suffice to wear a cross around the neck, or even to kiss it occasionally? Is it enough to go to church and sing hymns about the cross? Is it enough even to declare that it was at the cross that Christ saved us?

Is not one more thing necessary? A few days ago Paul told us that we are to have the same mind that was in Christ Jesus and led him to the cross. In another study he told us that we are to seek a share in his sufferings, becoming like him in his death. Thus, being a friend of the cross of Christ means that this cross is a subject not just of devotion but also of imitation. Being an enemy of the cross of Christ means refusing to participate in this devotion and imitation, rejecting what we do not like, making sure that we have an easy religion that does not lead to difficulties. Is that not what we are doing when we wear the cross around the neck and sing hymns about it, but do not live in a way that reflects the mind that was in Jesus?

Have you heard of cases of famous preachers who have constantly proclaimed the cross and by doing so have become multimillionaires, yet have refused to share with others? Is it possible, even while preaching the cross, to be among the enemies of the cross whose god is the belly? When we allow ourselves to be enticed by a message about a Christian life full of success and prosperity, with little or no suffering or sacrifice, is there not the possibility that we may be joining the enemies of the cross of Christ?

The same may be seen in another way in which this passage points to the same contrast: on the one hand, the enemies of the cross think only of that which is earthly; on the other, true believers have their citizenship in heaven. This does not mean that they are always looking at the sky, as if earth were not important. What it means is that they live in this world, whose god is the belly, as those who know that the last word belongs not to the belly or to a bank account or to popularity, but to the Lord, who is to come from heaven.

Imagine a parade with a loud band, and crowds marching to the same rhythm. Now imagine in that parade a few people who carry their own radios and earpieces and listen to a different tune. These people will march to a different rhythm. From the point of view of those who have organized the parade, they will be a disaster. But what is happening is not that they have no rhythm. They are listening to a different music, following a different band and a different director. That is what happens when our citizenship is in heaven. We can no longer march to the rhythm of the world, as if the belly were our god, or as if all this rubbish were true gain. Now we march to a different rhythm. That very fact may lead others in the parade to dislike us and criticize us and even to seek to expel us from the parade. Yet, this is the meaning of being a friend of the cross of Christ. Have you ever had such an experience, or do you know someone who has?

Act: One of the greatest difficulties in being a friend of the cross of Christ is that from the point of view of the rest of the world such a person seems crazy or out of rhythm. Try to think of people whose decisions have been a sign that, instead of thinking of earthly things and marching to the tune of the world, they look to heaven for their citizenship. Write down their names, and resolve that if at all possible you will seek them out to express your solidarity and admiration. When you have that conversation, ask that person to help you act in similar ways.

Or ask yourself: Am I a friend of the cross of Christ? Before you answer that question, think about an important decision you will have to make soon. What should that decision be if you are a friend of the cross of Christ? Write down your reflections in a few lines that will help you remember when the time comes to decide.

For Group Study

Invite the group to picture what has been said about the parade. Now describe the following hypothetical situation: Your congregation is in serious economic difficulties. You can hardly pay the pastor's salary or the electric bill. You do have a valuable ministry among the poor, trying to provide education, medical services, and legal aid. A large corporation offers you a huge amount of money, as well as another piece of property on the outskirts of the town, in exchange for your old building. If you move out there it will be more difficult or perhaps impossible to continue serving the poor. But you will have a beautiful church in a better neighborhood with ample parking and modern facilities.

Divide the group in two, one to propose that the building be sold, and the other that the building be kept. Give them a few minutes to discuss and rehearse the arguments for their positions.

Now bring the two groups together. Divide the blackboard or newsprint into two columns: "Arguments of the Enemies of the Cross" and "Arguments of the Friends of the Cross." Invite the entire group to list some of the arguments for their position and to try to decide under which of the two columns their arguments best fit.

W E E K

FOUR

First Day: Read Philippians 4:1.

See: This one verse is remarkable in that there are few verses in the Bible where the themes of joy and love are so dominant. Twice Paul declares that he loves the Philippians. When he calls them his "crown," he is referring not to a royal crown but rather to the laurel wreath that the winner of a race receives. Thus, Paul has returned to the image of an athlete running a race. But now the prize is not, as in 3:14, "the heavenly call of God in Christ Jesus," but rather the Philippians themselves, whom Paul calls his crown.

Among these many words of love and joy, Paul's one admonition stands out: "Stand firm in the Lord."

Judge: If while reading this verse you review what we have been studying during the last three weeks, you will note that there is hardly anything new here. Paul is simply repeating and reinforcing what he has already said about love, joy, unity, and the need to stand firm.

Paul's line of thought may be compared to a stairway. Paul does not call his readers to continue climbing at every step of the argument. Every once in a while, he offers us a moment of relaxation, very much like a landing on a stairway. Why do you think Paul does this? Think about what happens when you reach a landing in a stairway. You stop for a moment, breathe deeply, take a rest, and perhaps then you look back. You count the floors you have climbed and think about what still remains. In the case of this letter, which was intended to be read aloud in the church, the listeners had no way of knowing how much more was still ahead of them. But this "landing" would help them review what they had learned.

Quite likely the purpose of this verse is precisely that: to force us to take a breather and review what we have studied to this point, thus reiterating the central themes of the epistle: joy, love, and firmness in the faith.

Act: Look at your notebook and review what you have written during the last three weeks. Whenever you come across a decision or resolution you have fulfilled, pray, giving thanks to God. Whenever you read something where you have not followed through, pray, asking for forgiveness and strength. In the section for today's reflections, make a list of those resolutions still pending. End your session with a prayer, asking for strength and guidance along the way.

Second Day: Read Philippians 4:2-3

See: At that time, it was customary to place all greetings and concrete recommendations to individuals toward the end of the letter. This is what Paul does here, as he moves from more general assertions about the nature of the faith to concrete recommendations. It is here that for the first time we find the names of some of the Philippians.

Nothing more is known about Euodia and Syntyche than what Paul says here. The two names are feminine, so these seem to be two female leaders in Philippi. This is not surprising for, contrary to common opinion, in Paul's churches there were many women in positions of leadership. In this particular case, there seems to have been some disagreement between them. This may be one of the reasons that the entire epistle stresses unity. But even while calling them to unity, Paul commends them, "for they have struggled beside me in the work of the gospel." To what events this refers is not known. But there is no doubt that he feels respect and gratitude toward these two women, even though apparently they are now causing some problems.

There is no indication who it is that Paul calls "my loyal companion." Nor do we know anything else about "Clement and the rest of my co-workers." Our not knowing about them may not be all that important. What is important is that their "names are in the book of life."

Judge: After all that Paul has said about the need for unity and love one would expect him to respond with harsh words when he learns that two of the leaders in the church in Philippi are having serious disagreements.

Why do you think that, instead of having them expelled from the church or condemning them for not having understood the importance of unity, Paul recommends that they be helped? Is it not the case that, were Paul to attack and condemn them, he would be falling prey to the very lack of love and unity that he wishes his readers to reject?

Try to think of a concrete case in one of today's congregations. Perhaps sometime ago someone began saying or doing what was not correct. Soon that person met resistance from wiser, more faithful people. At the beginning, it was quite obvious who was damaging and dividing the church. But little by little the situation became bitter, to the point that eventually love and charity were abandoned by all. The question of who started the conflict was no longer important. Now bitterness and division preyed on all of them. This is what happens to one degree or another whenever, instead of helping those who err, we simply attack them without making every effort to call them to the right path on the basis of love and support. (Remember that in 3:18, where Paul finds it necessary to declare some to be enemies of the cross, he does this "even with tears.")

When someone in your church errs or is uncooperative or causes divisions, what are we to do about it? What do you do about it?

Act: Think of someone in your church who has been marginalized because of something he or she did or said. Pray for this person. Resolve to approach him or her and discover ways to be supportive and loving.

Third Day: Read Philippians 4:4-5.

See: Paul nears the end of his letter with a series of recommendations. The first of these, as the tone of the entire epistle leads us to expect, is Christian joy. He stresses this by repeating his exhortation: "Rejoice in the Lord always; again I will say, Rejoice." All that follows will be framed by this recommendation, for the Christian life, even in spite of all its difficulties, is a joyful life.

The word that verse 5 translates as "gentleness" could also be translated as "meekness," "pleasantness," or "tolerance." What Paul is telling the Philippians is that they are to behave in such a way that their affable and gentle character will be generally noted. This is not always a simple matter, for it is often easier to deal with others with harshness rather than with gentleness. This is particularly true when, as was probably the case with Philippian Christians, others around us are hostile. For this reason, Paul reminds them why they are to behave with gentleness: "The Lord is near."

In a word, believers are to rejoice and be gentle, not on the basis of their own effort but because they have a reason to rejoice that the rest of the world does not know: The Lord is near! This does not necessarily mean that the Lord is about to return once again; but it does mean that the Lord is always at hand, within reach of our call and our prayers.

Judge: Do you think that trusting that the Lord is near can help you follow Paul's exhortations?

Can you remember a time when you were a small child and were afraid of the dark? Do you remember when one of your parents told you, "Don't be afraid; I am here, even though you can't see me"? Even though the light was off, that near and trustworthy voice helped you overcome fear.

Isn't the same the case with life today? If we forget that the Lord is near, fear and difficulties will overwhelm us. If something does not turn out the way we wished, or someone criticizes or attacks us, we are carried away by wrath and bitterness. But if, on the contrary, we remember that "the Lord is near," everything takes on a different shape. Trusting that nearness gives us new strength and valor.

Act: Read or sing the hymn "Abide with Me," or at least the first stanza:

> Abide with me; fast falls the eventide;
> the darkness deepens; Lord, with me abide.
> When other helpers fail and comforts flee,
> help of the helpless, O abide with me.

Turn this into your prayer for today and whenever you feel overwhelmed by difficulties, sorrows, or doubts.

Fourth Day: Read Philippians 4:6-7.

See: Note that verse 7, which is frequently used as a blessing at the end of a service, is actually a promise. Paul promises the Philippians that "the peace of God ... will guard."

Paul tells the Philippians that this promise will be fulfilled as they follow the advice in verse 6, of letting their requests be made known to God. Note that they are told to go to God "by prayer and supplication with thanksgiving." In other words, they are to share with God their pains and concerns (in supplication) as well as their joys (in thanksgiving).

Judge: Throughout the epistle Paul commends sharing. This includes sharing with God (in today's passage) and with others (in the passage for the day after tomorrow).

Prayer is the main way in which we share with God both the good and the bad. We share the good in thanksgiving. We share the bad in supplication, placing our pains and concerns in the hands of God. Thanksgiving curbs our pride, and supplication curbs the power of anxiety.

Thanksgiving curbs pride because when we acknowledge that every good gift comes from God we can no longer glory in it as if it came from ourselves. If, for instance, we are proud because we sing well or preach well, that pride will be undercut when, in true thanksgiving, we come to acknowledge that these gifts come from God. If there is something in your life that tempts you to vainglory, that is the first thing for which you must thank God; then you will no longer be able to boast of it as if it were your own doing.

Supplication frees us from the power of anxiety, because it reminds us that we are not alone and that the solution for whatever causes us concern is not completely in our hands. If, for instance, a disease causes me anxiety, when I place my condition in the hands of God, anxiety loses its sting, and I enjoy "the peace of God, which surpasses all understanding."

Act: Jot down in your notebook the three or four things about which you are most anxious. Next to each of them write: "Lord, I place it in your hands."

Repeat this prayer as often as necessary until you feel the anxiety waning.

Now write down the three or four things of which you are most proud or with which you are most pleased. Next to each of them write: "Lord, it all comes from your hands."

Repeat this prayer until you feel that the power of pride is being overcome. During the coming days repeat these prayers so that the peace of God which surpasses all understanding will guard your heart.

Fifth Day: Read Philippians 4:8-9.

See: These two verses are a promise, like the two we studied yesterday. Yesterday's verses promised that "the peace of God . . . will guard your hearts and your minds in Christ Jesus." Today's verses also end with a promise: "and the God of peace will be with you."

Yesterday's promise had a human counterpart: the Philippians were to share everything with God in supplication and thanksgiving. Today's promise also has a human counterpart: what believers are to think about. While the long list may hide the center of the sentence (for instance, "whatever is true, whatever is honorable, whatever is just"), it all comes together at the end of verse 8: "Think about these things." In other words, believers are to think about a series of things: the true, the honorable, the just, the pure, the pleasing, the commendable, the excellent, and the worthy of praise.

Judge: Do you think it is possible to have control over your own thoughts? Obviously, in a certain sense it is not. If I tell you right now not to think about an elephant, no matter how hard you try to avoid it, an elephant will come into your mind, even if it is just for moment. And the more you try not to think about an elephant, the more you will think about one. Thus it does not seem possible to control our thoughts.

However, in this text Paul tells us to think about certain things, and, by implication, not to think about others. Therefore, there must be a way to control one's thoughts. The truth is that, although thoughts cannot be controlled in the short term, as when I tell you not to think about an elephant, they can be controlled through a discipline.

For instance, if we live in an atmosphere in which violence and uncontrolled sex are glorified constantly on television and in the books we read, eventually such thoughts will seem natural to us and will come to mind even at the least suggestion. If, however, we avoid participating in such entertainment, if we seek healthier books and television programs, it will be easier for us to avoid such thoughts.

If we find it difficult to think about the true, the honorable, the just, and the pure, is this perhaps a sign that we have allowed the surrounding atmosphere so to pollute our minds that it controls our thoughts?

Act: List in your notebook the things that Paul calls us to think about: the true, the honorable, and so on. Now review in your mind what you have done with your leisure during the last two or three days—TV programs you watched, books you read, conversations you had. If any of these activities led you to the sorts of thoughts that Paul commends, make a note of it. (For instance, if a movie made you think about justice, list it in your notebook next to "the just.") But if you recall activities that led you to thoughts or feelings contrary to Paul's list, make a note of them, if possible in red ink.

During the next few days, as you talk with friends and family, as you watch television, or as you choose your reading material, take a moment to review them in the light of Paul's list.

Sixth Day: Read Philippians 4:10-20.

See: This passage too is a promise, for Paul concludes telling the Philippians that God "will fully satisfy every need of yours." But the passage is also a summary of the argument of the entire letter, for it opens by speaking once again of joy. In this case, however, Paul's joy is over some concrete aid he has received from the Philippians, for his relationship with them is such that they are ready to send him support, and he to receive it.

As background for this relationship, read again the story of the early days of the church in Phillipi in Acts 16:9-40. There you will find two people who from the beginning shared with Paul what they had. The first of these is Lydia of Thyatira, who after being baptized with her family insisted on offering hospitality to Paul and his companions. As Acts 16:15 says, "she prevailed upon us." Apparently, her hospitality was such that Paul felt constrained to accept it. The other person in Philippi who shared with Paul and Silas was the jailer. We all know the story of his conversion. What we often forget is that even before being baptized the jailer washed the wounds of Paul and Silas, and that after being baptized he took them into his home and fed them.

It is interesting to note that Acts, where little is said of such things, gives us two examples in the particular case of Philippi of people who shared their goods with Paul and his companions. Reading now the Epistle to the Philippians we realize that the largesse of this church was still at work. (See also 2 Corinthians 8:1-5, where Paul uses the generosity of the churches in Macedonia as an example for the Corinthians to imitate. Remember that the church in Philippi was the main church in Macedonia.)

Finally, note that the passage ends with words of praise. Praise is an antidote against vainglory, for if the glory belongs to God it does not belong to the Philippians, nor to Paul nor to any of us.

Judge: Do you think that among Christians we share as much as we should? Think first of all in terms of feelings. The church should be the place where, since we are all one family, we can share our most secret feelings. Is this true of your church? Do you help make it so?

Now think of material goods. The Philippians shared their goods with Paul. Do we share enough among ourselves? When there is someone in need among us, do we offer concrete help or do we simply say that we are going to pray for him or her, as if that were all we had to offer?

Think now of your congregation's budget. How much of it is spent on the church itself, and how much is shared with the rest of the community? In the ancient church the offering was collected mostly for the needy. If there was hunger or if crops failed, the church fed the hungry. If there was an epidemic, the church invested its resources in public health, and Christians took care of the sick. Today we (the church) don't seem to do as much in that direction. Most of the resources collected by the church are spent on salaries, utility bills, building maintenance, and in other similar items. Could this be one of the reasons that the witness of the church is less effective?

Act: Repeat the exercise you did during the first week of this study: look at your checkbook and at the record of checks you have written. Write two columns in your notebook, one under the heading "For Myself and My Family," and another under the heading "For Others." List your expenses under each of those columns and add them.

Now look back in your notebook at the page where you did the same exercise the first week of this study. Has something changed? Do you now spend more than you did before for the benefit of others? Has your joy increased with your giving?

Seventh Day: Read Philippians 4:21-23.

See: The letter closes with a series of greetings. There is nothing extraordinary about this. It was customary to send greetings at the end of a letter.

What is indeed surprising in these verses is a few words that could easily go unnoticed: "especially those of the emperor's household." What is translated here as "household" could also be translated as "family." However, this does not necessarily mean that these were the emperor's relatives. At that time, the "household" or "family" included not only a person's relatives but also others who were dependent on the head of the household, including slaves and free dependents, who were usually called "clients." Therefore, being "of the emperor's household" simply meant that one was a slave or in some other way a dependent of the emperor.

Paul was in prison under the custody of imperial authorities. Therefore, it is quite likely that these "saints" who send greetings to the church in Philippi are part of the guard appointed to guard Paul. Somehow, these people have been so affected by his witness that they have embraced his faith and now send greetings to their brothers and sisters in Philippi whom they have never met.

Without any great fanfare, which might have endangered these "saints of the emperor's household," Paul is telling the Philippians that at least some members of his guard have been converted. Remember that quite possibly one of the Christians in Philippi was the jailer who had been converted after hearing Paul and Silas sing hymns while they were prisoners and seeing the power of God in an earthquake. This jailer, as well as the rest of the church in Philippi who knew his story, could read between the lines and rejoice in the manner in which Paul's witness has brought these members of the emperor's household to faith.

With these words, Paul closes the epistle by a clear example of what he has been saying from the beginning: that a joyous Christian life is a powerful witness to the faith. Without having to spell it out explicitly, Paul gives them an overwhelming proof of a joyful witness.

Judge: Do you believe there is a connection between joy and the power of a Christian witness? Look around you at the various Christian congregations you know. Is it not true that, in general, churches where the people go around with long faces, as if they were carrying the weight of the world, are churches that don't grow? Is it not true, that churches where it seems that people attend services out of obligation also do not grow? Is it not true that the churches that grow are those that express joy both in their worship and in their mutual relations?

There are two reasons for this. The first, fairly superficial explanation, is that people prefer being in joyful rather than gloomy, morose environments. But the second reason is much more important: If we say that the gospel is "good news," how then can we not feel and show joy? When people receive good news, they give signs of joy—they smile; they call a friend; they shout, sing, or even weep. When we say that we are proclaiming good news but give no signs of joy, it is difficult for those who see and hear us to believe what we say. If we do have good news, why are we not celebrating? Why do we not hasten to share the news with our friends and neighbors?

Think about your own faith community. The entire epistle is a call to Christian joy. (If time permits, you may wish to read again the whole letter, underlining every occurrence of words like "joy" and "joyful.") Is there joy in your faith community? Are you yourself joyous?

Act: The entire letter that we are now finishing underlines two themes: joy and sharing. Particularly in the passages we have been studying this week, we have seen that there is joy in sharing. Consider the possibility that Christian joy grows as it is shared. (Think of a bit of good news you have received. Did you not immediately try to find someone to share it with? Did this not increase your joy?) The experience of many believers has been that precisely in the act of sharing the good news of the gospel, the good news has gained particular relevance for them. Resolve that at least for the rest of this week you will take every opportunity to share the gospel. This does not mean buttonholing people and asking them if they are saved. It means rather explaining that your joy comes from knowing Christ. Show yourself to be joyful, and when people ask you why you look so happy, tell them.

Such resolutions, however, must go beyond generalities. Think concretely about some of the people you expect to see in the next few days and how you will show them your joy in the gospel.

Close this session by reviewing what you have written in your notebook during this four-week study of Philippians. Try to summarize what you have learned in one or two paragraphs.

For Group Study

In conversation with the group, try to find a place that seems to be in dire need of joy and happiness. (This may be a shelter for people with AIDS, a retirement home, a hospital, or a jail.) Make plans to visit that place, bringing with you joy, love, and hope. Do point out that one visit will not suffice to witness to joy. Joy is grounded in love, and love requires commitment.

If the group decides to visit some such place, it must make a commitment to go regularly and to establish bonds of love with people there. If you do not do this, your love will not be genuine (see Romans 12:9), and therefore your joy also will not be genuine.

W E E K

FIVE

First Day: Read Colossians 1:1-2.

See: Colossians is another of Paul's letters from prison. Yet it is very different from Philippians. The church in Philippi had been founded by Paul, who had strong personal bonds with some of its members. But the church in Colossae is never mentioned in Acts, and apparently Paul never visited it.

Colossae was a small city near two others that are also mentioned in Colossians 4:13: Laodicea and Hierapolis. Although formerly a fairly important town, by Paul's time it had declined significantly and was overshadowed by both Laodicea and Hierapolis. All that remains today of Colossae is a small hill on which a few ruins may be found.

Apparently the church in Colossae was founded by Epaphras (Colossians 1:7), and Paul wrote this letter either because Epaphras came to visit him in prison or because he was a prisoner with Paul. Epaphras let Paul know that some people were trying to introduce false teachings into the church in Colossae. Paul wrote this letter to refute those teachings, apparently at the request of Epaphras. Thus, this letter is more theological than Philippians. It is also less personal.

Judge: Reading this letter, especially after studying Philippians, we may be surprised that Paul takes the time to write to a church in which apparently he knew very few people and that was the result of someone else's ministry. But this points to one of the secrets of the extraordinary growth of the church in those early times: believers really considered themselves members of a single family and a single church.

Have you ever had the experience of unexpectedly finding a Christian brother or sister in a distant place? This is not such a rare experience among immigrants, particularly those who arrive in the new country without resources or work and perhaps even without proper documents. Many of them can tell stories of how someone they did not know helped them simply because of their common Christian faith.

An uncle of mine arrived in Miami penniless. He did not want a porter to carry his luggage, for he would be unable to tip the man. But the porter, seeing that my uncle was elderly and was not in good health, insisted on carrying the luggage, even though my uncle told him there would be no tip. As they walked they spoke of their faith. Upon arriving at their destination, the porter took a bill out of his wallet, gave it to my uncle and said: "My brother in Christ, today it is my privilege to tip you." I am certain that today my uncle and that porter, one a Cuban exile and the other a fairly poor African American, sing together in the heavenly choir.

Act: Review some of the good that has been done for you by sisters and brothers in the faith, unknown people who however love you for love of Jesus Christ. Perhaps someone provided a scholarship that made it possible for you to study. Perhaps you were in an accident and received someone else's blood. Resolve to do something for someone you do not know well or at all. Do it in remembrance of all you have received from others, and in celebration of the love of Christ that binds us with unknown brothers and sisters throughout the world.

You may wish to speak with your pastor seeking guidance as to how some of your financial resources may be used to help the needy either in your own neighborhood or in faraway places. The church has the necessary contacts to do this, and we do not use them often enough.

Second Day: Read Colossians 1:3-14.

See: At the time that Paul was writing it was customary after giving the name of the letter writer and greeting the addressees to invoke the gods, asking for the well-being of the latter. Here Paul does something similar, but at the same time very different. It is different, first, because Paul invokes not the many gods, but the one and sole God. It is also different because instead of asking for health and prosperity for his readers, Paul thanks God for what they have already received and asks God to grant them, not health and prosperity, but "knowledge," "spiritual wisdom and understanding" (1:9). Note that when Paul speaks of what the Colossians have received (1:4-5) he lists faith, love, and hope—the same list that appears in 1 Corinthians 13:13 but in a different order.

As we have already seen, and as will be explained more fully later on, the problem in Colossae that prompted Paul to write this letter was the presence of false teachings that threatened the very core of Christianity. This is why, when Paul prays for the Colossians, he asks that they may have knowledge, wisdom, and understanding—that is, that they will not allow themselves to be deceived by false teaching.

Note that this is important because it is the foundation so that the Colossians "may lead lives worthy of the Lord, fully pleasing to him, as you bear fruit in every good work and as you grow in the knowledge of God." In other words, the purpose of true doctrine is not just doctrine itself but also a life of obedience to God.

Judge: Why do you think Paul underscores the Colossians' need for wisdom, knowledge, and understanding? Sometimes we think that what is important in the Christian life is that we do good, that we have faith, that we try to be faithful. All of that is crucial. The problem is that if we err seriously in our understanding of the gospel we shall also err in our efforts to be obedient. Without "knowledge" of what the gospel is, without the "wisdom" necessary to live it out in different circumstances, and without the "understanding" to distinguish true doctrine from false, Christian obedience becomes very difficult, no matter how good our intentions.

Later in this study we shall see what was the Colossians' main error and how it relates to us in our situation. At present, however, ask yourself: *Now that I have been studying the Bible* systematically for several weeks, how has this helped me understand the gospel better? Has it helped me be more faithful, obedient?

Act: Since this passage shows us the importance of knowledge, wisdom, and understanding, it is a good time to evaluate your study so far. Ask yourself, *Have I been sufficiently faithful in my study? What obstacles have I encountered? Is the time I have set aside for study the best? Does it suffice? Is the place that I have assigned for my study the best?*

Think about changes that could make your study more effective. Write them down and make them.

Third Day: Read Colossians 1:15-20.

See: In this passage, Paul speaks of the Son to whom he referred at the end of the previous one. The Son is "the image of the invisible God." Part of what this means is that, although God is invisible, we can see God in the Son. The Son is also "the first-born of all creation." This means that the Son precedes every creature, and is not simply some latecomer. If we take into account the rights of the firstborn in antiquity, it also means that the Son has preeminence and sovereignty over all of creation.

The word "all" appears repeatedly in this passage, as well as throughout this epistle. One could say that, just as the key word in Philippians is "joy," the key word in Colossians is "all." Note that all created things, visible and invisible, earthly and heavenly, have been created "through him and for him."

In verse 16 Paul declares that among the things created through the Son and for the Son are "thrones or dominions or rulers or powers." These were names given to various categories of angels and other celestial beings. Some people believed that these heavenly beings ruled over the movement of the stars, and that through such movements they ruled also over human life. But Paul rejects such notions. If such beings exist, they too are created through the Son and for the Son. They have no independent authority. And most certainly they do not rule the world at their whim, as astrologers claimed.

Judge: It is quite common in our society for people, as they read the newspaper, to read also their horoscope for the day. Others believe that the sign of the Zodiac under which they were born somehow determines their destiny or their character. The notion behind such practices and beliefs is the same that Paul rejects in this passage: that in some mysterious way the stars control and determine human life.

What do you think Paul would say about this? He would certainly consider it a serious error, for it forgets that, if there are hidden powers, all of them, as well as the rest of creation, are less than the Son. For the Colossians, to believe that "thrones and dominions" controlled their lives was to deny the universal lordship of Christ Jesus. Could the same be true of us when we put our trust in horoscopes and in the hidden power of the stars?

Act: Are you among those who consult the horoscope? Are you among those who believe in seers, palm readers, tea leaves, Tarot cards, or similar things? In that case, read verse 16 anew. Ask yourself how these things relate to the lordship of Jesus Christ over all things. Resolve to leave aside such superstitions, which in the last analysis deny that lordship.

If you are not among those who consult such things, try to discover something in your life that threatens to take the place that belongs only to "the firstborn of all creation." This may be money, your personal prestige, or your work. These things are not in themselves evil. (Paul does not say that "thrones or dominions" are evil. What he does say is that they must be under the dominion of Christ.) What is evil is to grant them an authority and power independent from the lordship of Christ.

Make a list of these things that threaten to rule your life. Copy verse 16 but substitute the things you have listed for words such as "thrones," "dominions," or "rulers." Read it out loud and write down your reflections.

Fourth Day: Read Colossians 1:15-20.

See: You will note that this is the same passage as yesterday's. This is because this passage is crucial to understanding the message of Colossians. We noted yesterday that the word "all" appears repeatedly in Colossians. As you read today's passage, underline each occurrence of that word.

Apparently the false teachings that had made their way into the church in Colossae held that some things were under the authority of God and the Son, and others were not. Some things were creatures of the divine, and others not. Some things were the object of divine love, and others were not. Some things had a place in the divine plan, and others did not. This is why Paul insists that the Son is the first born of *all* creation through whom *all* things have been created. Furthermore, Paul stresses that this includes visible as well as invisible things, and those in heaven as well as those on earth. Even more, God's purpose is "to reconcile to himself *all* things."

In Paul's time there were many religions and systems of belief that held that invisible and immaterial things were good, and that visible and material things were bad. They held, for instance, that the soul was good but the body was evil. Apparently it was some such teaching that was circulating in Colossae and causing concern to Epaphras. Therefore, Paul underscores that *all* things have been made through the Son, who is to have preeminence in *all* things.

Judge: Have you ever heard doctrines similar to those that seem to have been circulating in Colossae? Some people think that God is interested only in "spiritual" things and that the body is of less concern to God. What do you think Paul would think about this? Would he not say that the body, just as much as the soul, is God's creation, and that the Son is to have the first place in both?

The "knowledge, wisdom, and understanding" that Paul wishes the Colossians to have and that we also should seek should show us that both body and soul are from God, that God loves both, and that we do not properly serve God when we concern ourselves with one at the expense of the other. When we do not have such an understanding, we risk being disobedient while believing ourselves to be very religious. Do you see a connection between this and the fact that so many Christians spend so much time going to church and praising God, while seeing no point in helping a needy neighbor?

Act: Look around you. Make a quick list of some of what you see: furniture, pets, gadgets, plants, and so on. Now think about some things that you do not see, such as air, spirit, mind, and so on. When you have a list of a dozen or so items, read it slowly, saying to yourself over each of them, "God made it. It is good. It belongs to God." End your session with a prayer: "I thank you, God, for your wonderful creation. I thank you for what I like. And I thank you for what I do not like. I thank you that it is all yours. And I ask you to give me knowledge, wisdom, and understanding, to use it all according to your holy will. Through Jesus, your Son, through whom and for whom all things were made. Amen."

Fifth Day: Read Colossians 1:21-23.

See: After referring to all the rest of creation, Paul now turns to the Colossians and says "and you . . ." As we read these words in the context of our studies for the last few days, this does not mean simply that the Colossians have now joined the Philippians, the Corinthians, and other Christians. It means much more than that. After telling them that *all* things are part of God's plan, Paul now tells the Colossians that they too are part of that God's creation and plan.

When we see this in the text, we realize that what Paul is telling the Colossians, and therefore also us, is that if something should surprise us it is that *we* are part of God's plan, that, in spite of what we are and have done, *we* too have reason to hope under the lordship of the Son through whom *all* things were created and in whom *all* things—even we—find their fulfillment.

Judge: Read the passage, changing the word "you" for "we." As you do this, think about your faith community and how the passage refers to you.

Now read the passage again, inserting your name after the word "you." Remember, as you read it, that these words appear in the context of a passage dealing with the cosmic scope of God's power and love.

Note also that in reading this passage you have to acknowledge that your reconciliation with God comes not from yourself but from God. Look at the second part of verse 21 and ask yourself how you "were once estranged and hostile in mind, doing evil deeds." You will note that here, as throughout his epistles, Paul stresses the divine initiative in human salvation.

Why do you think it is so important for us to acknowledge that our salvation comes through God's initiative and that we do not deserve the grace we have received? Could it be because only when we realize this can we truly accept and love people whom we might consider less acceptable or less worthy of love?

Think of the most unworthy person you know. Now read the entire passage remembering that this person is part of the *all* to which the passage refers. Think about how you can express this reality in your attitude and actions.

Act: Discuss with other people in your community of faith how you have been saved by sheer grace. Discuss with others how you might bring others to the same experience. Make specific plans to contact and invite some of the people in your neighborhood whom no one visits or invites. Remember that in doing this you are doing no more than what the Lord did with you and with every believer by coming to dwell among us and show us his love.

Sixth Day: Read Colossians 1:24-25.

See: Once again, as before in the epistle to the Philippians, we encounter the theme of joy. This should not surprise us if we remember that both epistles were written at approximately the same time and from the same place.

Here, as in Philippians, this joy is not necessarily lack of suffering. On the contrary, Paul declares that he is "now rejoicing in my sufferings for your sake." His sufferings are the motive for his joy. This does not mean that he likes to suffer; rather it means that he is aware that he suffers for the good of the Colossians and other Christians.

The notion that Paul is "completing what is lacking in Christ's afflictions for the sake of his body" is astounding, for it would seem to imply that Christ's sufferings were not complete. But that is not what Paul means. Paul is suffering what is still lacking in the sufferings of the body of Christ, the church. Paul rejoices that he is suffering so that the body of Christ may be built up.

It is to that suffering church, which still has more to suffer, that Paul has been made a minister. His service to the church includes both announcing the word of God and suffering for that word and for the church itself.

Judge: Do you think that Paul enjoyed suffering? Why does he say that he rejoices in his sufferings? Have you ever rejoiced in your own sufferings, not because you liked them but because they were a respite for another? If you are a parent, remember your wakeful nights with an ailing child. You did not enjoy staying awake, but you did it gladly and even rejoiced in the opportunity to do it, out of love for your child.

There are people around you who suffer. Is there anything you can do to take part of their burden, as Paul did for the church? Think of two possible cases:

First, a single mother in the church is ill and has difficulty caring for her children. Is it possible for you to lessen her burden, even though it might mean increasing yours?

Second, in a field near you people working on the harvest are underpaid and living in unhealthy conditions. They are trying to unionize in order to improve their working conditions. If you support them, many will criticize you and even resent it. Is there any way in which you can at least begin to take some of the burdens of these people?

Act: Find near you some group or individual who suffers because of human injustice, disease, or some other reason. Think about how you could relieve the burden of such people. Consider also the cost to you in time, worries, and perhaps even criticism. Write down the cost you might expect. Pray about it, and if you come to a decision write the following in your notebook: "Help me, Lord, to lessen the sufferings of _____, even though this may cost me some suffering."

Seventh Day: Read Colossians 1:26-29.

See: The word of God which Paul proclaims is a "mystery that has been hidden throughout the ages and generations but has now been revealed to his saints." It is important to take some time to study these words in light of the cosmic outlook of this particular epistle. We have already noted that, just as the characteristic word of Philippians is *joy*, in Colossians it is *all*. Philippians looks upon things, so to speak, from here below and deals with the joys and sufferings of believers; Colossians looks at the big picture, as if Paul and his readers were spectators looking upon the drama of the ages. This drama includes all things visible and invisible, things heavenly and earthly. It includes also all the times "throughout the ages and generations." That great cosmic drama is the "mystery" that has now been revealed to God's saints—to Christians. What Paul affirms here (and, as we shall see later, also in Ephesians) is that all of creation has been made in and through the Son, that all of history revolves around the mystery of the coming of the Son, and that this mystery that is the key of creation and history is that Christ is in us "the hope of glory."

Thus, Christ is not only the savior. He is also the beginning and the end of creation. That is why the word *all* is so important in this epistle. To forget it, as if Christ were the beginning and end only of some things, is to limit his lordship. To claim that there are things that are not part of what was created through the Son implies that there is another creator, another principle, and therefore another goal.

This is why Paul proclaims Christ, as he says in verse 28. But it is also the source of the power in Paul's proclamation. Note that at the end of our passage Paul declares that he acts "with all the energy that he powerfully inspires within me." According to Colossians this energy is the same power through which all things were made, visible and invisible, on earth and in heaven, throughout the ages and generations. It is not surprising that Paul's proclamation is effective, with such power behind it!

Judge: Do you think that what we believe about the Christ whom we serve makes any difference for our Christian life? Suppose, for instance, that you believe in a Christ whose power is limited to only a part of creation; would you then go to the rest of creation in order there to proclaim and serve him? Or would you stay where you are, the only place where you seem to be secure under the protection of the Lord? If Christ is like a tree protecting us from the searing sun of a hostile desert, then we are quite justified in trying to remain under his shade and not venturing forth. Or suppose that your Christ is creator and redeemer only of souls but not of bodies. Would you devote as much energy to healing sick bodies as you do to saving lost souls? Or would you insist that the business of the church is souls, and that the care of the body is to be left to others? If we believe that Christ is Lord only of the spiritual world, we are surrendering the material world to the Enemy.

When in your church people speak of the mission of the church, or of the responsibilities of the faithful, are they speaking of a Christ who is "the first born of all creation," so that "all things have been created through him and for him"? Or is the talk really about a smaller Christ, whose work is limited to part of creation?

A brother declares: "I am a Christian, I attend church regularly, and I support it with my offerings. But how I spend the rest of my money, and on what, is my business." What such a brother is actually saying is that he believes in a Christ who may be Lord of other things, but not of his goods or his bank account.

A sister says: "I am a Christian, but don't expect me to forgive what Sister So-and-so did to me." What she is actually saying is that her Jesus may be Lord over everything, but not over her feelings.

A pastor says: "What you believers have to do is come to church, support its programs, and contribute to its expenses." That pastor is actually saying that Jesus Christ is Lord of the church but not of the rest of the world and of life.

We all have aspects of our life that we wish to withhold from the lordship of Jesus. For some of us it is money; for others, a job; for others, family life; for others, certain political convictions. No matter what it may be, as long as there are segments of our life over which we reserve the right to rule, we have not totally understood the import of Paul's words to the effect that Christ is "the firstborn of all creation, ... the head of the body, the church, ... the beginning, the firstborn from the dead, so that he might come to have first place in *everything*."

Act: In a way, today's study is a review of what we have studied during this week, and in particularly of the meaning of the word *all* in Colossians. Therefore, begin by reviewing this week's study, in particular what you have written in your notebook.

Now ask yourself what are some areas in your life where the lordship of Jesus Christ is not manifest. Make an inventory of such things and write down your thoughts about them. Think for instance of money and how you manage it, of how you spend your time, of your own work and how much good it does for others.

After reflecting on each of the things that may still not be under the lordship of Christ, spend some time praying quietly that he will take them and rule over them.

For Group Study

Invite the members of the group to read slowly the first chapter of Colossians, underlining every occurrence of the word "all." After all have completed this exercise ask them why they think this word appears so many times in the text. You may try reading the entire chapter out loud, but saying "some" where Paul says "all." The contrast and the importance of "all" will be clear.

Ask the class to consider which of these two readings really expresses our faith and the way we live. Is it possible that we say we believe in the "all" but live under the "some"? Lead the group in a discussion about what aspects of life we keep for ourselves, without allowing Christ to have the first place. The discussion should include aspects of personal life (money, family relations, career, and so forth) as well as elements in the life of the church (how it makes its plans, sets its budget, appoints its committees, and so on).

If time allows, list those aspects of life where we have most difficulty relinquishing the lordship to Christ. Choose one of these and ask the group to discuss what would happen if Christ were the ruler of this aspect of our lives. What would change? What would be the consequences of those changes? Could it be that the reason we reserve this area of life is that we suspect what the consequences would be, and we fear them?

W E E K
SIX

First Day: Read Colossians 2:1-5.

See: Paul declares that he is "struggling." The nature of that struggle is not clear. Apparently Paul had never visited either Colossae or Laodicea, the other city mentioned here. Nor is there any indication that Paul is actually fighting with someone in particular. Apparently, his struggle is more emotional and spiritual. Perhaps it would be better to translate this passage in the sense that Paul is "agonizing" over these two churches. Paul is pained by the knowledge that the churches in Colossae and Laodicea have been invaded by false doctrines that threaten the very core of the gospel. In short, the picture we should have before us is Paul in prison, ardently praying for the well-being of these churches and trying to determine what he will tell them that may strengthen them against the danger that threatens them.

What Paul does is to insist on the contrast between true knowledge and the teachings of those who seek to "deceive you with plausible arguments." Apparently, the false teachers who had come to these cities claimed to have a special wisdom, a secret knowledge, of the divine mysteries. This is why Paul uses these very words, but in a different sense. He tells the Colossians that he hopes they will "have all the riches of assured understanding and have the knowledge of God's mystery, that is, Christ himself, in whom are hidden all the treasures of wisdom and knowledge."

Then in verse 5, Paul declares that he rejoices "to see your morale and the firmness of your faith." Though, as he has just said earlier, the believers in Colossae have not seen him "face to face," he is with them in spirit. Thus, while obviously concerned over the false teachings that are seeking to penetrate the church in Colossae, Paul does not think that the believers there have accepted such teachings.

Judge: Through the discipline of the Bible study you are following, you will learn much more about biblical teachings. Concretely, this study of Colossians should help us all understand that the lordship of Jesus Christ reaches much farther than we often imagine.

It is quite likely that as you read Colossians you will discover that some of the beliefs, practices, or attitudes of people around you are similar to those of the false teachers who had come to Colossae. In that case, how will you respond? Will you allow false teaching to prosper, simply to avoid unpleasantness? Will you attack them in such a way that your own life will be embittered, thus leading you also into error? What does Paul's example teach us regarding false doctrine? Note that Paul's struggle is not against the false teachers themselves. His struggle is against false doctrine, and he responds to it with both correct doctrine and true love.

Act: Our best action in the face of the text we are studying is to pray. Pray, first, that God will help you grow in wisdom and in the knowledge of truth. Pray, second, that God will help you distinguish between secondary matters, in which error has no major consequences, and really fundamental issues, in which error may lead the faithful and the church astray. Pray, third, for those who teach or accept doctrines that truly deny or threaten the very gospel of Jesus Christ. And pray, finally, for yourself, that God may help you oppose such false doctrines with wisdom and with love, with firmness and with gentleness.

Second Day: Read Colossians 2:6-15.

See: Paul continues calling the Colossians to remain firm in the faith and reject the false doctrines that are seeking to infiltrate the church. Even though he is not with them, the Colossians are to continue living in Christ just as they have received him.

False teachers sought to convince believers "through philosophy and empty deceit." Apparently they claimed that believers had to be circumcised, and this is why Paul tells the Colossians that they have been "circumcised with a spiritual circumcision." It is also quite likely that the false teachers called believers to fear evil spiritual powers, such as "the rulers and authorities"— terms that were often used for such powers. This is why Paul tells them that Christ has "disarmed the rulers and authorities and made a public example of them."

Since in Christ "the whole fullness of deity dwells bodily," the doctrines of these false teachers—that there are things out of the scope of the lordship of Jesus—must be rejected. Concretely, to claim that circumcision is still necessary is to forget what Christ has achieved.

Furthermore, since Christ "is the head of every ruler and authority," and since Christ has defeated them, there is no reason to fear them.

Judge: The text we are studying warns us against two dangers. First of all, there is a danger that we might think that what Christ has done does not suffice and that we therefore need to trust in our own actions or holiness for our salvation. Second, there are believers who think that, although Christ is Lord over all, one should hedge one's bets and seek protection in one's own power, financial schemes, or perhaps even superstitious practices.

These two dangers seem to oppose each other, for one seeks a stricter form of Christianity and the other is not willing to trust Christ as final Lord of all. What joins the two is that both dislodge Christ from the center. Legalists put their laws in the place of Christ. The others place their fears above the power of Christ.

Are you in danger of being swayed by either of these misunderstandings? Are you one of those church members for whom Christianity is simply a series of strict laws, as if it were more important to obey those laws than to trust in the grace of Christ? Or are you one of those who, while calling themselves

Christians, put such trust in other things that it shows they are not really sure of the absolute lordship of Jesus?

Act: Remember that the central theme of Colossians is the word *all*. Review your life and actions during the last few weeks. Have they shown that Christ is *all* for you? Are you convinced that Christ is the first-begotten of *all* creation, in and through whom *all* things have been made?

Pray: "Lord, help me trust in you and only in you. Give me the faith so that I will not lean on false gods or put my final trust in anything but Christ and his power. It is in his name that I pray, for it is the name that is above *every* other name. Amen."

Third Day: Read Colossians 2:16-17.

See: Note that the word *anyone,* which is so prominent in verse 16, is parallel to the *no one* in verse 8 and to the *anyone* in verse 18, which we shall study tomorrow. In contrast to the *all* that appears throughout the epistle, Paul here underscores the *no one.* The one is the counterpart of the other, for it is precisely because *all* have been created in Christ that *no one* (nor anything) has the authority to lead us away from him with false teachings or with superfluous requirements.

In the two verses we are studying today, Paul warns his readers against the legalistic inclinations of false teachers. Yesterday we already saw him warning believers against those who claimed that physical circumcision was necessary. Now we see him rejecting the notion that in order to be faithful it is necessary to fast on certain days or abstain from certain foods or observe particular festivals or insist on particular days of rest. Paul acknowledges that all these requirements were part of the ancient law given by God to Israel. But it was "only a shadow of what is to come." The reality behind that shadow is none other than Christ. Once he has come, the shadow is no longer binding.

Judge: How shall we respond to those who tell us today that in order to be faithful to Christ there are certain observances of the

Old Testament that must be kept? There are, for instance, those who insist that the day of rest must be a certain day of the week, or that there are foods from which Christians must abstain. We may try to refute such people on the basis of Bible quotations or rational argument. But our fundamental argument must be that any who place such observances and doctrines at the center of their faith dislodge Christ from that center. This should serve as a warning to us, because if in order to win the argument we end up placing another doctrine or another biblical text at the center of our faith, we shall have gained nothing. The center belongs to Christ, and only to him.

For many reasons, some of them quite valid, it is common among Christians in this country to insist on the evil of alcohol, gambling, dancing, and tobacco. Some raise these issues to the level of absolute requirements for the Christian faith. How are we to respond to such attitudes? Are we to accept such views? If we do not accept them, how can we reject them while at the same time acknowledging the evil that may sometimes be connected with alcohol and the rest? In all this, how are we to show that Christ is the *all*?

Act: Imagine that you are a person who insists on the matters mentioned above as absolute requirements for the Christian life. On the basis of the passage we have just studied, what do you think Paul would say to that? Write that response in your notebook.

Imagine that you respond to such people by calling them fanatical legalists who do not understand the workings of modern society. What do you think Paul would say to that? Write down that response also.

Fourth Day: Read Colossians 2:18-23.

See: Paul continues warning the Colossians against doctrines that displace Christ from the center of all things. Once again, these false teachers claim to know secrets about the angels and other such subjects that it is impossible for humans to know.

Paul summarizes these teachings with the phrase "Do not handle, Do not taste, Do not touch." Over against this, what true Christians are to do is to hold "fast to the head, from whom the whole body ... grows with a growth that is from God." Once again, the false teachers do not accept the lordship of the Head over *all* things. According to them, there is a different source, an evil one, for those things that are not to be handled, tasted, or touched.

Paul makes it very clear that such teachings are attractive, for they have "an appearance of wisdom." They seem to promote piety and humility. But in truth they do not check self-indulgence.

Judge: Why do you think that Paul declares that to abstain from certain things as if they were evil in themselves is no more than a human command and teaching? Could it be that there is within our hearts the desire to turn the free love of God into something we have earned? Could it be that there is something within our sinful nature that rebels against the notion that salvation is a free gift of God and therefore leads us to try to earn it? Could it be that we like such rules and regulations because in fulfilling them our inordinate pride is fed?

If the false teachers to whom Paul refers are guilty of trying to turn the free gift of God into something they have earned, are we perhaps guilty of the same? Are we not doing that when we invent rules and more rules?

Act: Think about the last paragraph you have read. Seek to apply it directly to yourself and not primarily to others. Finally, pray: "I glorify you, Jesus Christ, my Lord, because in you the fullness of God dwells. I thank you that you have earned for me a victory that otherwise would never be mine. Teach me to trust in you, and only in you, who are the all in all. Amen."

Fifth Day: Read Colossians 3:1-8.

See: Today's study takes what we have been discussing to a more practical level. Up to this point, the main thrust has been that, if Christ is all in all, this has certain implications for the doctrines we hold. Now we shall see that it also has far-reaching consequences for the life we lead.

Paul expresses this thought in two different ways. One we shall study today, and the other tomorrow. In today's passage, Paul establishes the relationship between the new life in Christ and the fact of having died and risen with him. In an earlier passage, Paul tells the Colossians that "when you were buried with him in baptism, you were also raised with him through faith" (Colossians 2:12). Now he applies this to Christian living. Dying and being raised with Christ is not only a promise of life after death; it is also a matter of a new life here and now.

The apostle Paul says it quite clearly: Christians are dead, and our true life is hidden with Christ, awaiting his final manifestation. This means that Christians ought to live, not as those who remain in the old life, but rather as those who have truly died to the values, principles, and goals of that other life. Being dead, Christians must kill whatever there is in us that is a remnant of the old life.

Judge: What do you think is the meaning of having died in Christ? Is it possible to be a Christian without somehow being dead to the old life? What are some signs that we ought to give of this newness of life?

What signs can you give (what signs *do* you give) that your life is hidden with Christ?

Act: List the things in verse 5 that Paul says that Christians are to put to death. Scratch out those that have really died in your life. Underline those that you do practice or that still tempt you.

Pray over each of these, saying: "Lord, in the cross you crucified my _____. Do not allow that which you have killed to continue living in me. Amen."

Sixth Day: Read Colossians 3:9-17.

See: Yesterday we saw Paul expressing the need for Christ to be at the center of Christian life by using the image of having died in Christ and having one's life hidden in Christ. Now Paul turns to a different image, that of dress. One who has left the old life has "stripped off the old self with its practices," and one who has received the new life is "clothed ... with the new self."

Note that Paul repeatedly speaks of being "clothed." First, in verses 9 and 10, he speaks of being clothed in the new self, "which is being renewed in knowledge according to the image of its creator." Then, in verses 12 and 13, he speaks of being clothed with a series of virtues. Finally, in verse 14 he tells the Colossians that above all they must "clothe yourselves with love." In a way, this reminds us of the much more extensive passage in 1 Corinthians 12 and 13, where after speaking of a variety of gifts of the Spirit, Paul declares that he will show "a still more excellent way" (1 Corinthians 12:31), and then goes on to his famous hymn on love. Likewise here in Colossians, after listing many virtues, Paul declares that the best way of being clothed with Christ is love.

Judge: There's an old saying "You can't tell a book by looking at its cover." In Spanish we mean the same when we declare, "A habit does not make a monk." What we mean is that appearances are often deceiving and that dress is not sufficient to enable others to know the character of a person.

Still, however, dress is important. In ancient times soldiers wouldn't go into battle without some sort of armor. Obviously, the main purpose of wearing armor was not to gain respect as a good soldier but rather to have protection against the arrows of the enemy. Today, players on a sports team wear uniforms. Wearing uniforms does not make them better players nor does it protect them from their opponents, but it does help them recognize each other. Finally, we all know that we feel better about ourselves when we are well dressed than when we are not. We know that our worth is the same, but still we do feel better when we are dressed appropriately for the occasion. When we are wearing clean clothes we try not to step in the mud.

In these examples, dress has three functions: (1) it serves as a defense against the enemy; (2) it helps us recognize those who are on our side; and (3) it gives us a sense of dignity that keeps us away from filth.

Consider each of the virtues Paul commends in the verses we are studying. How does it serve as a defense against the enemy? How does it help us know other Christians? How does it give us a sense of worth that keeps us away from uncleanness?

Act: In your notebook, list the virtues that Paul commends. Rate yourself on each of them on a scale from 1 to 10. Resolve to work on those virtues on which you scored low. Plan to look again at this page in a few days to make note of your progress. Do remember, however, that your worth and your salvation are the result not of your virtue, but of the love and grace of God.

Seventh Day: Read Colossians 3:18–4:1.

See: We now come to a passage that has been much discussed, for it deals with, among other things, relations between spouses. However, before we jump to conclusions about what Paul says, we should study the passage carefully and within the context of the social structures of the time. (Later in these studies we shall look at a parallel passage in Ephesians.)

Note first of all that here Paul speaks of three pairs, or sets, of relationships among people: first, between spouses; second, between children and fathers; third, between servants or slaves (in Greek there is a single word for both) and their masters. In Greco-Roman society, all of these were very unequal relationships, and in order to understand the text we must know something about them.

First of all, marriage, the first of the three relationships that Paul discusses, was a very unequal relationship. The husband was the head of the household, not only in the sense that his word was final, but also in the sense that all property and children were his. It would be very hard for a woman to divorce her husband—and only if she had the support of other males, such as her father, representing her interests. But the husband could easily divorce her by simply deciding to do so. In such a case, the wife could not raise any legal objections, or claim part of the family property or any sort of alimony. Furthermore, the children belonged to the husband, and a divorced mother had no right to them. Although in some circles physical violence on the part of a husband was frowned upon, it was not illegal. Over against her husband, a woman had almost no rights.

The relationship between fathers and children was also quite unequal. Children remained under the *paterfamilias*—the chief male of the household—not only while they were young, but as long as the *paterfamilias* lived. Only he could have property, so that, strictly speaking, whatever children made belonged to the older chief of the household—who did not even have to be their father but could be a grandfather or an uncle. Fathers had the right of life or death over their children. Furthermore, in traditional Roman society, when a child was born the father had no obligation to accept it. By simply refusing to make the symbolic gesture of picking up the infant, he condemned the child to be abandoned outdoors, there to die or be picked up by someone else. This was quite legal and relatively common. Before a father, a child, no matter how old, had practically no rights.

The same was true of the relationship between masters and slaves. If a slave killed a master, all slaves of the deceased were to be condemned to death, even if at the time they were hundreds of miles away. Legally, slaves, just like children and wives, could not own property. (There were slaves who did own property, but thanks only to the goodwill and permission of their master.)

Furthermore, there were strict laws limiting the conditions under which a master could free a slave. Even then, a slave was not "free" in the strict sense, but was rather a "freedman" or "freedwoman," which was an inferior condition to those who were born free. Only the children of freed slaves could be called "free." But even they had to remain as "clients" of the head of the household—the *paterfamilias*—to which they belonged, and this condition placed on them certain obligations that the truly free did not have.

It was in the context of that society and those conditions that

Paul wrote the words we are studying regarding relationships between husbands and wives, fathers and children, masters and slaves. When we take this into account we notice that what Paul asks of each of the weak parties in those relationships is no more than what society required of them: wives should be subject to their husbands; children must obey their fathers; and slaves their masters.

However, what Paul says to the powerful party in each of those relationships is surprising and even revolutionary in that social context: husbands are to love their wives and never treat them harshly; fathers are not to provoke their children; and masters are to treat their slaves justly and fairly. Even more, masters must remember that they have a Master! Masters are servants or slaves of a higher Master, who commands them to be fair with their own servants!

Judge: Imagine that you are a married woman in that society of the first century. Your husband, who abuses you, is also in the congregation. What will you think when you hear Paul's words? What do you think your husband will hear?

Repeat the same exercise, imagining now that you are the husband. Do likewise imagining yourself a father, a child, a slave, and a master.

Does it now seem to you that Paul is conservative in his comments, or that he is revolutionary?

Act: Begin by writing down your reflections on the above questions.

Now consider an unequal relationship in which you find yourself. Think first of a situation in which you are the one in authority—for instance, if you are a boss, a pastor, a parent. In that unequal relationship, what do you think Paul would say to those who are subject to you? Write it down. What would Paul say to you? Write that down also.

Repeat the exercise, but thinking now of a relationship in which you are the person subject to another. What do you think Paul would tell those above you? Write it down. What do you think Paul would tell you? Write that down also. Now consider what this implies about your attitude and behavior in such relationships. Write down your conclusions and resolve to follow them.

For Group Study

Divide the group in half. Assign to one group the roles of husband, father, and master; and to the other, the roles of wife, child, and slave. Make certain all understand what is said above regarding the obligations of each of these persons in the society of the first century. When all understand their roles, read the passage from Colossians out loud, asking the powerful to hear as such, and the powerless to do likewise. After the reading, ask the group to discuss what each heard according to the role assigned to them.

W E E K

SEVEN

First Day: Read Colossians 4:2-4.

See: Paul calls on the Colossians to pray earnestly. Remember that at the beginning of the letter he tells them that he is praying for them. Thus, Paul is calling them to do what he already does. In reading these verses while remembering the beginning of the letter, we note a reciprocity in prayer: Paul prays for them, and they are to pray for him. Furthermore, they are to pray with thanksgiving, which is exactly what earlier he had told them he was doing.

Note, however, that the Colossians are not to ask that Paul be freed from prison, as he and Silas (who is the same Silvanus who is writing the letter jointly with Paul) were freed in Philippi. The "door" that they should pray for God to open is the door to witnessing, so that Paul and Silvanus may be able to "declare the mystery of Christ." What they should ask for Paul is that he may be able to reveal that mystery clearly.

Judge: Is there a relationship between the mutual bond of prayer binding Paul and the Colossians and the unity of the church? Note that Paul does not claim to have particular authority over the church in Colossae. It is not a church he founded. Yet, Paul and the Colossians are part of the same church. Could they be such if they did not pray for one another? Is it possible that unity among Christians begins when we truly pray for one another?

Paul asks the Colossians to pray not for his freedom, but rather for the freedom of the word. Is this what we usually desire when we ask sisters and brothers in the church to pray for us? Do we want them to ask God to help us fulfill our mission, proclaim the gospel, give witness to God's love? Or do we actually ask that they pray for our problems to be solved, our hurts healed, and our finances prosper?

Act: Consider what Paul asks of the Colossians, even when he is in jail. He asks them to pray, not that the door of his prison may be opened but that somehow a door may be opened for preaching and witnessing.

Now imagine that next Sunday you will have a chance to ask for the prayers of the church. Try to follow Paul's example. Write down what you would ask the church to pray for in such a case by completing the following: "Sisters and brothers, pray for me, so that _____."

Close your study session praying what you have just written.

Second Day: Read Colossians 4:5-6.

See: Paul has just spoken of his own witness, and now in these two verses he speaks of the witness of the Colossians toward "outsiders," that is to say, the pagan population of Colossae. The first thing Paul tells them is that they must walk "wisely" in their relationships with such people. This advice probably has several dimensions.

First, remember what Paul has written a few verses before regarding unequal relationships. This is probably a call to the Colossians to proceed wisely in such relations. For instance, a slave who knows that Christ has freed him should not allow this knowledge to poison his relationship with the master, thus bringing upon the church and its preaching unnecessary difficulties.

Second, it means also that Christians are to make certain that their witness is clear. They are to walk wisely before outsiders so they will not even be suspected of deceit or immorality.

Finally, Paul's words probably mean also that Christians are to be wise in their witness in the sense of not being impertinent, insisting on calling others to conversion who are not even ready to listen to them.

Wise Christian witness means "making the most of the time." More traditional translations say "redeeming the time." We often understand this as if Paul meant that we should always be occupied. However, this is not the exact meaning of the phrase. Possibly a better translation would be "making the best use of timely opportunity." In other words, the Colossians' witness before pagans is to be presented at the opportune time, without letting that time pass but also without unwise impertinence. This is part of what Paul means by telling them to behave "wisely" toward their neighbors.

Finally, Paul says that the speech of the Colossians is always to be "gracious, seasoned with salt." The first means that this word is not to be cutting, bitter, or condemnatory. The second means that it is to be a pleasant word, perhaps even with a bit of humor.

Judge: Do you think that it is possible for a word of witness to be true but not wise? Suppose, for instance, that someone comes to you asking for help in an urgent matter of life or death and instead of responding to that request you tell the person to wait and listen to your word of witness. In that case, your witness, even though true in its content, may turn out to be very false in its implications. At the same time that you tell the person of God's love, you postpone the opportunity to show that love.

Review some of the evangelistic sermons you have heard recently, either in church or through the mass media. Were they wise as well as true? Did the attitude of the preacher reflect God's love and compassion? Would outsiders hear primarily a joyous word of grace or an angry word of condemnation? Was the speech "seasoned with salt," or did it take itself so seriously that there was no gentleness or humor in it?

Act: Think of a nonbeliever with whom you interact repeatedly, perhaps a fellow worker, a relative, or a neighbor. Review the opportunities you have had to share your faith with this person.

Did you do it wisely? If not, where did you fail? Were you able to make "the most of the time"? When you talk about religion with this person, do you do it with grace and a bit of salt, or with dogmatic rigidity? Jot down your reflections and plan for a way to speak to the person with greater wisdom.

Third Day: Read Colossians 4:7-9.

See: We now come to the final greetings in the letter. At that time it was customary to close a letter with greetings to the readers from all who were with the writer.

The first greetings come from Tychicus and Onesimus. Tychicus was from the province of Asia, possibly from somewhere near Colossae. He was to be charged with the task of delivering the letter that Paul was just closing. Something similar is said about him in Ephesians 6:21. He was to go to Colossae both to bring the believers there a word of consolation and to bring them news about Paul and his companions. He would later return to Paul bringing news from the Colossians.

Onesimus was a slave who had run away from his master Philemon, a believer in Colossae. He and Tychicus are to travel to Colossae taking Paul's letter to the believers there as well as a shorter and more personal note to Philemon.

Judge: Have you ever thought that in a way Tychicus is as important for the Epistle to the Colossians as Paul himself? Without Tychicus the epistle would not have reached its destination. Perhaps Paul would not even have written it, not having a way to be certain that it would be delivered. However, hardly anyone ever remembers Tychicus.

I am a writer, and I often think of all the publishers, editors, printers, distributors, and bookstores without which my writings would never reach the public. Although my writings bear my name, in truth their existence owes as much to all these people as to me.

Quite often something similar happens in the church. There are some people whose work is acknowledged, perhaps because it is more visible. But this does not make them more important than the rest. Furthermore, without these unnamed persons the work of the more famous would be lost—as the Epistle to the Colossians would have been lost without Tychicus.

Act: In your congregation, are you like Tychicus, whose work is scarcely noticed? Or are you like Paul, whom others acknowledge as a leader? If you are like Tychicus, do not be discouraged. Tychicus carries the letter not in order to be thanked, but in order to serve. His service is of the greatest importance, even though few acknowledge it. Give thanks to God for your opportunities to serve, even without recognition. If you are like Paul, think of the many "Tychicuses" around you without whom your work would not be as effective. Thank God both for the opportunity to serve and for all these other people who make your service possible.

As you reflect on these matters, jot down your thoughts.

Fourth Day: Read Colossians 4:10-18.

See: Today's study concludes our reading of Colossians. In this passage salutations continue. The various names that appear here could well serve as starting points for many reflections.

Aristarchus was a native of Macedonia, possibly from Philippi, where he met Paul. He then went with Paul to Asia Minor, and finally went with him when he was imprisoned and sent to Rome for trial (see Acts 19:29; 20:4; 27:2).

Mark, Barnabas's relative, went with Barnabas and with Paul on their first missionary journey, but then abandoned the enterprise. When Paul and Barnabas planned a second trip, Barnabas wished to take Mark with them, but Paul refused. As a result, Paul and Barnabas went their separate ways. Mark's presence with Paul as this letter was written shows that they were eventually reconciled.

Of "Jesus who is called Justus" no more is known than what Paul says here.

We have already seen that Epaphras may be the same as the

Epaphroditus who appears in Philippians and Philemon. Epaphras was a leader and perhaps the founder of churches in Colossae and the surrounding area. If he is Epaphroditus, he delivered the Philippians' offering to Paul.

"Luke, the beloved physician" has traditionally been identified as the author of the Gospel of Luke and the book of Acts, although this is by no means certain.

These were the people accompanying Paul. Several of them are also mentioned in the Epistle to Philemon.

Then Paul sends greetings to the believers in Laodicea who apparently are expected to read this letter, "to Nympha and the church in her house," about whom no more than this is known, and to Archippus, whom we shall meet again as we study the Epistle to Philemon.

In the last verse Paul says that he writes this greeting with his own hand, indicating that he dictated the rest of the letter and that he physically wrote only these last few words.

Judge: Remember that, as far as we know, Paul had never been in Colossae. Apparently some of his companions did know the believers in Colossae. In general this is a correspondence between people who did not know each other personally. In spite of this, they exchange warm greetings. The church is a network of love, so that all members are joined together.

Is this still true today? Do you remember your brothers and sisters in distant regions? What do you know about those who belong to other denominations? Does your congregation encourage people to establish contacts and relations with members of other Christian communities, both near and far? Would this not enrich the faith of all?

Act: Resolve to establish close contacts at least with: (1) a believer in your own community who belongs to another denomination; (2) a believer in another town; (3) a Christian in another country. If you do not know how to do this, ask your pastor, or the board of missions in your denomination.

Fifth Day: Read Philemon 1-3 and 23-25.

See: We have read the first and the last verses of this brief letter, because here we have the names of all the people Paul greets as well of those who send greetings. The letter is sent personally to Philemon, and therefore most of it is in the singular form of address. But it is also addressed to Apphia, who may well have been Philemon's wife, and to Archippus, who may have been their son but who is also a leading figure in the church, as we learn from Colossians 4:7. Those who send greetings are Epaphras (or Epaphroditus, whom we have met repeatedly these last few weeks), as well as Mark, Aristarchus, Luke, and Demas, whom Paul calls "my fellow workers."

Apparently, Philemon and his family lived in Colossae, and therefore this personal letter addressed to him accompanied the more public one addressed to the entire church in that city.

Judge: Paul is about to ask an important favor from Philemon. As we shall see later on, he dares ask for this favor because their relationship is such that he could even command Philemon to do what he wants. It is on the basis of this relationship that Paul can intervene on behalf of Onesimus—as we shall see in two days.

Do you think Paul would have been able to write this letter without having some previous contact with this family?

Act: Review what you resolved yesterday. Do you think your life would change if you were really convinced that you had sisters and brothers throughout the earth? Reaffirm yesterday's resolution and ask for necessary help in fulfilling it.

Sixth Day: Read Philemon 4-7.

See: As in the other letters we have studied, after the initial salutations Paul adds a word of thanksgiving. In this particular case, he gives thanks for Philemon, as well as for the news he has received of him and of his faith. While giving thanks for Philemon, Paul also prays for him. It is in this context of thanksgiving and petition that Paul places the rest of the letter in which he will request from Philemon something of great importance.

Judge: Do you think that Paul's giving thanks for Philemon and praying for him was only a formality, that he did so because it was a convenient and traditional way to begin a letter? Or is it that the practice of approaching others with thanksgiving and prayer helps our relations with them? What do you think would happen if, whenever you approached someone, you gave thanks for that person, at the same time asking God's blessing on him or her?

Act: Try it. Make a list of the people with whom you expect to interact tomorrow, probably including your family, fellow workers, clients, neighbors, and so on. Think about each of these people until you find something for which to be grateful. Besides giving thanks, also pray for that person. Continue in that spirit until you have your actual meeting with each of these people. The results will surprise you.

Seventh Day: Read Philemon 8-22.

See: What we are studying today is the main body of Paul's letter to Philemon. In order to understand this letter we must remember what we learned last week about slavery in the ancient Roman world, and particularly about the laws governing it. It is because we do not know such laws that we often ask why Paul does not tell Philemon simply to free Onesimus.

Within the legal system of the Roman Empire it was a difficult matter to free a slave. There were even laws forbidding it, except in exceptional circumstances such as when a slave saved his master's life. Even then, the former slave was not "free" but rather "freed," and there was no possible way of moving beyond that condition. The children of a freed slave were "free clients" of the former master or his heir, but an ex-slave could not move from the condition of being "freed." This condition still required a certain obedience and services to the former master. Therefore, the legal act of freeing a slave did not make that person free as the master was. The former slave would forever remain inferior and subject to the former master.

When we take into account these laws and circumstances, what Paul tells Philemon is extraordinary and even radical. The law stipulates that Philemon can punish Onesimus severely for having fled and that if somehow he manages to free his former slave, Onesimus will still be tied to his service as a "freedman." What Paul requests and requires of Philemon is that, no matter what the law says and no matter what Onesimus's legal status may be, Philemon is to receive him and deal with him as a brother, as his equal.

It is important to underscore Paul's request because in the nineteenth century those who defended slavery frequently appealed to this epistle saying that Paul returned Onesimus to his rightful owner. What these people did not take into account is that Paul sent Onesimus back, no longer as a slave but as a brother, even though there was no provision in the legal system of the time for what Paul told Philemon to do.

When we study the text more carefully, there are some points that deserve note:

First, in verses 8-9 and 21, Paul tells Philemon that he is not commanding but rather pleading. Yet at the end, he says that he is "confident of your obedience."

Second, in verse 10, Paul speaks of "Onesimus, whose father I have become during my imprisonment." This has led many to think that Onesimus was a prisoner jointly with Paul. But this is not necessarily the case, since Onesimus may have been working in the prison, and Paul may even have been able to move about, as was sometimes the case with Roman prisoners.

Finally, in verses 10-11 there is a play on words. The name "Onesimus" means "useful" or "beneficial." Therefore, what Paul says could be translated as "I am appealing to you for my child Useful, whose father I have become during my imprisonment. Formerly he was useless to you, but now he is indeed useful both to you and to me."

Judge: The Epistle to Philemon draws little attention today, for we tend to think that it refers to the treatment of a slave, and since slavery is now a matter of the past (at least in our society) the epistle has little to say to us. However, when we study this letter we learn much about reconciliation and relations among Christians.

The letter is a beautiful example of such reconciliation. The law clearly stipulates that Philemon can do with Onesimus as he pleases. As a subject of the Roman Empire, Philemon has no obligation whatsoever to deal with Onesimus in a particular way. But as a believer he does have another obligation. Paul instructs him to receive Onesimus no longer as a slave but rather as a brother, and that if there is something for which Onesimus should pay, Philemon should not charge it against him.

Is there is a more relevant lesson for our Christian life today? In many of our churches people harbor resentment against others for past events—some that took place years ago. They are convinced (and sometimes they even declare) that they will not be satisfied until they take revenge. But the fact is that whether or not they take revenge, they remain bitter and resentful.

Sometimes we hear such people say they "have the right" and that what the other person did is "unforgivable." And there is no doubt that this is the case in the present social order: if others wrong us, we are justified in paying them back.

But what Paul says here is quite different. Perhaps within the social order we have the right to seek revenge, just as within the order of his time Philemon had the right to punish Onesimus. But the social order in which we live is not to be the order of the church. Onesimus has become a Christian; he has accepted the Lord. As a result, no matter what the law says, he is Philemon's brother, and Philemon is to deal with him as such. Whatever Onesimus did no longer counts, for Philemon himself knows that his own debts forgiven by God are much greater than Onesimus's. Thus, the first thing that this epistle tells us is that reconciliation with God in Christ implies and requires reconciliation with our own debtors.

There is more. Even were Philemon to forgive Onesimus's wrongdoing, there would always be a distance between them. Philemon was a master. We do not know how many slaves he had, but he certainly was not poor. As for Onesimus, even if Philemon were to forgive him he would still be nothing more than a slave. This is what the social order of the times expected.

But since the church is not a mere image of the surrounding social order, Paul tells Philemon to receive Onesimus as a brother, or as he would receive Paul himself. The social distances that the world dictates no longer count. Now Philemon and Onesimus are brothers. They are equals.

In some of our churches, even though we may forgive one another, we do not deal with one another as equals. We are still divided by differences of class, education, nationality, race, culture, and so on. We accept as members of the church people who are different, and we even give them the title of "brother" or "sister." But these are no more than titles, for they are still considered inferior or at least different and therefore distant.

What do you think Paul would say about this?

Act: The reconciliation that this letter expects has at least two important dimensions. The first is forgiveness. Paul asks Philemon to forgive Onesimus. Whoever keeps resentment and old hatreds has not been reconciled. Yet, we all know that such negative attitudes are among the most frequent evils in our congregations. As a response to this situation, ask yourself concrete questions about your need and readiness to forgive others. Questions such as:

Did someone say or do something to me for which I have not forgiven him or her?

Did someone oppose something that I proposed, and now I deal with that person distantly and with resentment?

If your response to these and other similar questions is yes, your best course is to ask forgiveness, first from God and then also from that other person.

The other dimension of this reconciliation is that it overcomes social barriers. Philemon was a master and Onesimus a slave, but now Paul entreats and orders Philemon to deal with Onesimus as he would with Paul himself. Even though in the surrounding society Philemon was more important than Onesimus, this difference must not be transferred into the life of the church.

In today's society there are barriers similar to those that existed then between masters and slaves. Too often these barriers exist also within the church. Ask yourself: What separates us one from another? Social standing? Different levels of economic status? Race? Different levels of education? Different ages and generations?

Ask yourself as concretely as possible: Are there people in my congregation on whom I look down because they belong to a different group, or do not dress as well as I do, or because they know less, or for any other reason?

Refrain from answering this question too quickly. Think it through. Make a mental list of people around you. When you think of a person on whom you look down for whatever reason, write: "_____, I receive you, no longer as a _____, but as my own brother (or sister)."

After writing as many names as necessary, and thinking about what you have written, pray: "You, Lord, who have forgiven us so much so that we might be reconciled with you, teach us to forgive so that we might be reconciled with others. You who came from heaven to become like the most humble among us, destroy the barriers among us. Amen."

For Group Study

The leader will know the group and its circumstances and therefore should be able to deal with this lesson with wisdom, tact, and firmness. One possibility would be to begin with a discussion about what Paul tells Philemon: to forgive whatever Onesimus owes him. After some time of discussion, make a general comment about the need for us to forgive one another. Then invite the participants to spend some time in silence to think about someone in the congregation or in the community whom it is difficult for them to forgive.

At the end of that time of meditation, allow any who wish to do so to express their thoughts. End by inviting all not only to forgive the people about whom they thought, but also to approach them and give them signs of love and understanding.

W E E K

EIGHT

First Day: Read Ephesians 1:1-2.

See: In our study of Paul's epistles from prison, we now come to the longest one. We shall focus our attention on the new life in Christ as it is discussed in this letter. You may have read commentaries claiming that this letter was written not by Paul but rather by one of his disciples. I am not of the opinion that these arguments are fully convincing, and therefore, in this study, I shall continue referring to Paul as the author of this letter. It is not a matter of great importance, but I mention it in order to avoid confusion or surprise if you find a New Testament scholar claiming that this letter was not written by Paul.

You may also find commentaries declaring that it is not certain that this letter was actually addressed to the Ephesians. These doubts are more convincing, for the oldest manuscripts we have do not include the words "in Ephesus" in verse 1, but actually say "to the saints and faithful in Christ Jesus." Some scholars suggest that this may be the lost letter that Paul wrote to Laodicea (see Colossians 4:16). Again, this uncertainty has little import for the message of the letter itself, but it is good to know.

If we now turn to the passage for today, you will note that in verse 1 Paul declares himself to be "an apostle of Christ Jesus by the will of God." This is crucial for understanding Paul's letters and ministry. He is not a self-appointed apostle, nor is he somebody who simply volunteered for the job. He is an apostle "by the will of God."

Judge: Francisco Franco, the Spanish dictator of the twentieth century, called himself "leader of Spain, by the grace of God."

When someone claims that he or she has a certain position "by the will of God" this tends to arouse suspicion in us. This is why we hesitate to declare that whatever we are doing is the will of God.

However, the very purpose of our study during these weeks is to discern the will of God for ourselves, for the church, and for the world. It is not only Paul who is what he is "by the will of God." Each believer must seek to discover what she or he is to be by the will of God. After all, that is what the Christian life is all about: living by the will of God. How then can we avoid the outrageous pride of a person like Franco, or of the pastor who claims things have to be done in a certain way because it is the will of God?

During these weeks of study, what have you learned that can help you discern the will of God for you?

Act: Review your notes from the seven weeks that have past. You may find there some help in answering the question that has just been posed. For instance, you will find that doing the will of God requires thanksgiving and intercession for others; that it requires acknowledging the lordship of Christ over *all* things (Colossians); that it requires joy and sharing (Philippians); that it involves righteousness, freedom, and new relationships (Philemon). Above all, you will discover that discerning the will of God requires that there be in us the same mind that was in Christ Jesus (Philippians 2).

Pray, asking that during the six weeks still remaining in this study you may discern God's will for you more clearly.

Second Day: Read Ephesians 1:3-14.

See: In the original Greek text, these twelve verses are a single sentence. This is the longest sentence in the entire Bible. The NRSV divides it into seven sentences. This is because in English we are not used to such long sentences, and have difficulty following them. By dividing the passage into a series of sentences, the translators have simplified our reading and comprehension of it. What is lost is the strong impression of a rolling and unstoppable stream that the original text conveys. What the NRSV gives us drop by drop so that we can assimilate it, in the original Greek is like a Niagara whose stream overwhelms us without allowing us even the respite of a period and a new sentence.

Dividing the text into several shorter sentences (which are still quite long) helps us understand it. But read it first as it was originally written, all at once and without stopping, and this will help you feel the main thrust of the text.

In fact, the text is a great hymn of praise. All that it says follows from the initial words: "Blessed be the God and Father of our Lord Jesus Christ."

Everything else, even though quite helpful for detailed study, is there first of all as a hymn of praise to this God and Father of our Lord Jesus Christ. That is why the text is written as it is. Its main purpose is not really to provide us information on predestination, sanctification, or salvation by grace. Its purpose is rather to carry us away in a hymn of praise. If it speaks about the time before the foundation of the world and the time after the end of history, it does so not that we may speculate about such times, but rather that we will praise and bless the Lord of all times.

This is why today you are invited to read the text without stopping. If there is something that you do not understand or that puzzles you, do not worry about that now. Simply listen to the text as you would to a symphony or a hymn.

Judge: Think of the Christian life as a great hymn. Sometimes we pay so much attention to each note that the melody escapes us. It is certainly good to stop every once in a while and reflect on specific elements of our lives. But sometimes we simply have to let the music move us, without stopping to study each note.

Think about the world and its entire history in this way. The text we are studying expresses that entire history as if it were a great symphony. As in the case of a symphony, we do not have to understand every detail in order to enjoy and celebrate it. Could it be that the reason Paul can speak of joy even while he is in prison is that for him all of life and history are like a great symphony directed by God? Could it be that when we praise God as this hymn does we are empowered to be joyful and faithful even in the midst of our tribulations?

Act: Read the first three stanzas of the hymn by William Cowper, "God Moves in a Mysterious Way":

> God moves in a mysterious way
> His wonders to perform;
> He plants his footsteps in the sea,
> And rides upon the storm.
>
> Deep in unfathomable mines
> Of never-failing skill
> He treasures up his bright designs,
> And works his sovereign will.
>
> Ye fearful saints, fresh courage take;
> The clouds ye so much dread
> Are big with mercy, and shall break
> In blessings on your head.

Pray that the words of this hymn may shape your life in such a way that you may be truly joyful as you bless the God and Father of our Lord Jesus Christ.

Third Day: Read Ephesians 1:3-14.

See: We are studying once again the passage we read yesterday. But now we shall pay particular attention to verse 3.

Note that this verse sets the tone for the entire passage, which is "a doxology," that is, an expression of praise to the glory of God. Although the passage is thick with doctrine, its purpose is not so much to teach doctrine as to praise God. That is why it begins with the words, "Blessed be the God and Father of our Lord Jesus Christ, who has blessed us."

Note also that the blessing is first of all God's. God "has blessed us." This is why Paul can say "blessed be God." Paul's praise is a hymn of gratitude for blessings received. It is not a petition for greater blessing.

The very word "blessing" requires some explanation. There are two different Greek words that the Bible translates as "blessing." The first really means happiness, as in the Beatitudes, "Blessed are...." This might be better translated as "Happy are...." The other word literally means "to speak well of." This is the meaning of the word "benediction" (*benedictio*). In this sense, God's blessing is a good word that God speaks over someone or something. The same is true when we bless. Since God's word always comes true, God's good word over someone or something also becomes a gift.

Thus, in this passage we are invited to speak words of praise to God because God has pronounced over us a good word, a word of salvation. This is why, in response to this good word of God, we are called to praise God.

Judge: Remember that God's Word is creative. In Genesis, when God says, "Let there be," things leap into existence. In the first chapter of John we are told that all that exists was created by the Word of God. This is why when God blesses (bene-dicts) the good that God speaks becomes a reality. (The opposite is also true, by the way. To curse is to speak ill of. This is the origin of the word "malediction.")

Is it not true of our own words that, even on a lesser scale, they also have the power to create and to shape? When we speak ill of someone, could we be contributing to making that person evil? When we speak good, are we not contributing to a person's goodness? Could this be why the Bible calls us repeatedly to bless and not to curse? (See for instance Matthew 5:44 and Romans 12:14.)

Act: Review what you have said about others during the past week. How many of your words have been of blessing, speaking well of others? How many have been of malediction, speaking ill of others? Resolve that, at least during the coming week, when you cannot say something good about someone, you will simply remain silent. Or even better, seek to find something good to say about everyone you meet and everyone whose name comes up in conversation.

Fourth Day: Read Ephesians 1:3-14.

See: We are still on the same passage. But now look particularly at verses 9 and 10. Here we find a subject that is characteristic of the epistle: mystery. Just as the main theme of Philippians is joy and the main theme of Colossians is "all," the main theme of Ephesians is mystery. Of the eighteen times that Paul uses this word in all his letters, seven are in Ephesians (1:9; 3:3, 4, 5, 9; 5:32; 6:19).

Regarding these verses, there are at least three points worthy of particular note. The first is that the mystery to which Paul refers, even though it has now been revealed, has not lost its mysterious character. Ephesians tells us that now we know that the will of God, God's plan for the fullness of time, is to gather all things in Christ. But it does not explain how this is to be. The mystery is revealed; but it is not explained away. Now we know what the ultimate will of God is; but how that will is to be fulfilled remains an impenetrable mystery.

The second point to be noted is that Christ plays a fundamental role in the fulfillment of the divine will. It is in Christ that the mystery has been revealed to us. But even more, Christ himself, bringing all things together, is the core of the hidden purpose of God. Christ is not only the revealer of the mystery, but also its fulfillment.

Finally, one must also note that this mystery involves the entire creation. God's purpose is "to gather up *all* things in him, things in heaven and things on earth" (verse 9). Here Paul shows the same concern that is central in Colossians.

Judge: The text is difficult not only because it is a long sentence but because mystery is at its very heart. How will these things be? We do not know. What we do know is that God's eternal design includes *all* things. It includes me, sinful as I am. It includes all of us who are following this study. But this is just the tip of the iceberg. It includes everything. It includes things in heaven and things on earth. It includes souls and bodies. It includes people, and also animals, plants, and even inanimate things. It includes individuals, families, communities, nations. It includes what now exists as well as what existed ten centuries ago.

How such a thing may be I cannot tell. But that is what the text actually says. No wonder we are told that it is a mystery. It is the mystery of mysteries!

Why do you think it is so difficult for us to accept the phrase "all things"? Could it be that our faith is too narrow, that we tend to limit God to ourselves and particularly to our souls? Could it be that our God is too small?

Act: Pray: "Thank you, Lord, that your will is so much greater than anything I could imagine. Thank you that the mystery of your will has been sufficiently revealed for me to know that I am included in your eternal redeeming design, and that I am one of the 'all things' that are to be united in Christ. And thank you, because, although I cannot comprehend the mystery, you lead me to trust in it. Take me in your arms. Lead me where you will. Do with me as you will. Because whatever you will shall be infinitely better than the best I could dream. Amen."

Fifth Day: Read Ephesians 1:3-14.

See: We continue studying this all-encompassing passage that begins speaking about things "before the foundation of the world," and ends with the consummation of all time.

Today pay particular attention to verses 12 and 13. Note two words that appear there: "you" and "we." This is another of the central themes of Ephesians: the relationship between Jews ("we") and Gentiles ("you").

The church, which originally had been entirely Jewish, was becoming increasingly Gentile. This produced disagreements, doubts, and debates. Some Jews who had been converted to Christianity resented the Gentiles, whom they saw as latecomers and second-class believers. Some of the converted Gentiles felt that they had now taken the place of the Jews.

What Paul says throughout the letter is that the center of our faith is Christ. Jew or Gentile, all are saved through Christ and in Christ. Furthermore, since the purpose of God is to unite all under Christ, those who despise others reject that purpose and are therefore drifting away from Christ.

Judge: As things have evolved, those who were "you" in Paul's time have now become "we." Today the vast majority of members in the church are Gentiles. The few Jews who do join the church are joining what is basically a Gentile institution.

But similar situations still exist. In many churches there is a dominant group, representing a particular culture, race, or social class. They are the new "we," and the rest are "you." As a Latino, I often find some people in my own denomination referring to the church as "we," and to Latinos, even within the same church, as "you."

What do you think Paul would say about this identifying as "we" and "you"? If the mystery of the gospel is that God's design is to unite all things in Christ, how does this fit with our distinctions between "you" and "we"? Is not part of the gospel the good news that even those who have come late have the same place as those who were there earlier? That the first comers have no right to claim privileges denied to the latecomers? The good news is precisely that we are part of God's purpose thanks to the grace of God who has blessed us in Jesus Christ, and not thanks to anything we have done or are.

Act: Ask yourself which of the following two descriptions best matches you:

• I have a tendency to think that, because of my race or culture or whatever other reason, I am not as valuable as the rest of the members of my church or denomination, and that I should be thankful that they allow me to be part of the church.

• I have a tendency to think that Christianity really belongs to people like me, of my race or culture, and that others are to be treated as welcome guests in a church that is really ours.

Now ask yourself how your attitude must change in the light of what Paul says in the passage we are studying. Resolve to value yourself as one who is indeed part of God's great design. Resolve to value others in the same way.

Sixth Day: Read Ephesians 1:3-14.

See: Today we complete our study of this very rich passage. Pay particular attention to the last two verses, where Paul speaks of the Holy Spirit.

Note that here Paul says that those who have believed have been "marked with the seal of the promised Holy Spirit." This refers to the ancient practice of putting a mark on an animal or a thing (and quite often on a slave) as an indication of ownership. This is still commonly done with cattle. Thus, being "sealed" by the Holy Spirit should be understood as being "branded" by the Holy Spirit.

This brand or seal is both a sign of the promise we have received and the beginning of its fulfillment. Paul says that the Spirit "is the pledge of our inheritance." In today's common language, we would say that the Spirit is the down payment of our inheritance. Thus the Spirit both affirms our hope and empowers us to live out of that hope. The Spirit is our foretaste of the coming reign of God.

Judge: Do you know churches or groups that speak quite often of having the baptism of the Holy Spirit, but where there is constant bickering, where people are treated unfairly, and where there are few signs of the sharing of which Paul speaks in Philippians? What would it mean in that situation to live as those who have received the down payment of the reign of God? If we truly have that Holy Spirit who is the pledge of the coming reign, how is this to be shown in our lives? What should be the signs of the Spirit in the community of believers? Remember that the main characteristics of God's reign are love, peace, and justice.

Act: On the basis of the questions that have just been posed, consider what you can do to give clearer signs that you actually live as one who has received the foretaste of God's reign. Write down your answers. Resolve to follow them. Ask God to help you do so.

Seventh Day: Read Ephesians 1:15-23.

See: Now Paul gives thanks for the faith of his readers. Note that this first chapter of Ephesians follows a similar order to the other letters of Paul we have been studying: Paul first identifies himself and his readers. He then has a word of praise to God (which in this particular epistle is the long doxology that we have been studying this week). Finally, he prays for his readers.

As in the other letters, this is a prayer both of thanksgiving and of petition. Paul gives thanks for the faith of his readers. But he also prays that they will receive such gifts as "a spirit of wisdom and revelation," that the eyes of their hearts be enlightened, and that they "may know what is the hope to which he has called you."

Judge: While studying Colossians, we saw that Paul was concerned about the false teachings that were circulating in Colossae as well as about a limited view of the lordship of Jesus Christ, which placed some things under that lordship and others not. Can you see similar concerns in this passage? Read the passage, underlining the words that have to do with knowledge, understanding, wisdom, and the like. Read it again, underlining in a different color the words that emphasize the fullness of Christ's lordship, words such as "all" and "every."

Do you see a common line of thought between this epistle and Colossians?

Act: Think of your greatest fear (this could be someone else, disease, death, poverty, a particular sort of animal). Write it down in your notebook.

Now write in your notebook the quote from verse 22: "He has put all things under his feet." Copy the phrase again, but now instead of "all things," write what you fear. (For instance, "He has put cancer under his feet.")

Read what you have written. Read it again, until its connection with the good news of the gospel and with the passage we are studying becomes clear. Pray, asking God to help you believe what you have written and to give you signs of God's power over what you fear. Decide to act as one who knows that the enemy has been conquered, that the last word belongs to the Lord.

For Group Study

Invite the group to review out loud what they have learned during the last week.

After that review, point out that today's text includes the phrase "and for this reason." The NRSV places this phrase in the middle of the verse so that the reason is what Paul has heard about his readers. But other versions place that phrase at the beginning of the verse, so that the reason of which Paul speaks is the entire doxology that precedes, and it is because of that doxology that he gives thanks for his readers.

In any case, there must be some connection between the doxology and today's passage. Read it slowly, inviting the group to comment at each point on the relationship between this reading and what we have studied during this week.

Perhaps the most important relationship, which you may wish to underscore, is that in the doxology the great mystery that has been revealed is God's plan to unite "all things." In today's passage Paul prays that his readers may be able to understand that God has put "all things" under Christ's feet. In both cases, what is important is the vast scope of the work and power of Christ.

W E E K

NINE

First Day: Read Ephesians 2:1.

See: This verse sets up a contrast between the old life of the Ephesians, which was actually death, and the new life of which Paul will be speaking. Twice in the early verses of chapter 2 we are told that we have been made alive. Such new life does not come as a result of something we have done, nor is it the development of a good seed in us. On the contrary, it is life that comes in the midst of death. It was when we were dead through "trespasses and sins" that Christ gave us life.

Judge: You have probably heard quite frequently about the new life in Christ or about a second birth. It is important to keep in mind that this life is so new that it comes in spite of being dead and buried in sin. This implies two very important points: First, that when we have sinned and are dead in our sins there is always the opportunity for rebirth. Second, that the same is true for everyone else, no matter how great their sin. Since there is forgiveness for me, I must always remember that there is also forgiveness for others.

This point is made quite clearly in Jesus' parable of the unforgiving servant, in Matthew 18:23-35. There, Jesus tells the story of a king who forgave one of his subjects who owed him an enormous amount. Later, this man who had been forgiven so much met one who owed him a pittance, but he was not ready to forgive that debt. We are all subjects whom the king has forgiven even though our debts were enormous. We are like dead people to whom the Lord has given new life. All this we have received, not because we were good, but simply by God's grace.

And now, when we see somebody who is still a debtor, who is still dead in sin, how dare we claim that the forgiveness we have received is not also available for that person? And yet, that is precisely what we often do.

We belong to the church, and we are proud of our faith and our good works. But if someone who is a notorious sinner comes to church or meets us somewhere else, rather than receiving that person with open arms, we reject him or her as a sinner. If this is what we do, Jesus' parable fits us and we should ponder it.

Act: Pray: "Help me, Lord, always to remember that if I live in spite of all my sins and all that I have done or left undone, it is only because you in your love have given me life in the midst of death. Help me remember also, when I see someone else who is dead in sin, that the life that you have given me and the love that you have shown me is also for that other person. Amen."

Second Day: Read Ephesians 2:2-3.

See: Paul continues speaking of the contrast between the old life that is not really life and the new life in Christ. Here, he speaks mostly of the old life. "The ruler of the power of the air, the spirit that is now at work among those who are disobedient," is none other than Satan himself. It is he who directs "the course of this world."

Note that being dead in sin is not something reserved for those who are particularly evil, but is rather the natural condition of every human being. Referring to himself and to others like him, Paul says, "We were by nature children of wrath, like everyone else."

Note finally that evil resides not only in "the desires of flesh and senses," but also in thoughts and attitudes. Paul does not think that the body is bad and the mind is good, but rather that the entire human being is sinful.

Judge: There is a dimension of the new life that quite often we forget, but that is also important. The new life requires the end of the old. It does not suffice to say, "I accept Jesus Christ," and then keep on living as before. If the old life was death, it is necessary to die to it.

This is why the text speaks of the course of the world that is led by Satan. That course or stream—as that word can also be translated—is powerful and tempting. But those who have died to the old life must no longer be carried by that course.

Here is an example: Last week we studied the case of Philemon and Onesimus. The "course of this world" would make us believe that slaves should continue being slaves, and that a runaway slave should pay for running away. But Paul tells Philemon otherwise. The "course of this world" tells us that if someone has hurt us we have the right to even the score. Yet in the order of the new life we know that we are only sinners to whom much has been forgiven, and that therefore we have no right to "get even" with anyone else.

Last week we thought about someone with whom we have had difficulties, and we resolved to seek reconciliation with that person. Have you done it? Or have you allowed yourself to be carried by the course of this world?

Last week we also looked at social barriers (also part of the course of this world), and how they infiltrate the church. What have you done to overcome such barriers?

If we still allow ourselves to be carried by the "current of this world," can we really claim to be born again by the power of Jesus Christ?

Act: Write down in your notebook a particular aspect of the "course of this world" that you still find attractive. Pray, asking God to destroy this aspect of your old life and strengthen your new life in Christ.

Third Day: Read Ephesians 2:4-7.

See: These verses underscore God's mercy and love, in contrast to our sin and death. As we saw earlier, God has given us life even when we were dead. Verse 5 dwells on this subject, affirming that God "made us alive together with Christ." Note that in this case Paul relates the new life of Christians to the resurrection of Christ. Christ also was dead, and God raised him from among the dead. We have new life not because of something we have done, but because we have been raised with Christ; because even in our being dead, God has given us new life. The same God who gave life to Jesus when he was dead has given us this new life. The message of Easter is that in Christ we have new life.

Judge: Do you believe it is possible for someone to commit such great and numerous sins that redemption is impossible? That is what we would like to believe, because then we could consider ourselves better than others.

However, this text says exactly the opposite. No one has sinned so much as to be beyond redemption. There is always the possibility of new life. This is why the text stresses that this life comes in the midst of death, and that this happens only by grace. New life is not as if someone who had apparently drowned has been revived. That person was not really dead. New life implies, as in the case of Jesus, being dead, truly dead, dead for three days, and then being alive. It is by sheer grace. It is not a matter of our still having a spark of life or a little goodness. It is rather that while we were dead Christ gave us new life. When there was nothing in us but sin, Christ redeemed us.

This is important and must be constantly preached, taught, and experienced, because without it we miss the real goodness of the good news.

Act: We have repeatedly seen the need of acknowledging that even those who seem most sinful are not beyond the reach of redemption. Think about someone you know who in your opinion is quite distant from God. Write down that person's name. Pray for him or her. Resolve that, as soon as you have an opportunity, you will show this person that there is still hope for newness of life. Keep praying for him or her throughout these weeks of study.

Fourth Day: Read Ephesians 2:8-10.

See: The epistle continues on the same subject. Salvation is by grace. Note that "grace" has the same root as "gratis." Grace is always free. St. Augustine used to speak of a "grace given gratis." Just as no one but God can draw life out from death, we cannot give ourselves new life. The result of this is that "no one may boast."

But even though salvation is by sheer grace this does not mean that there is nothing for us to do. God has given us new life in Christ so that we may be able to do "good works, which God prepared beforehand to be our way of life."

Judge: Upon finishing your study of this portion of scripture, review what we have studied throughout this week. New life is not just a second chance; it is a truly new mode of living. We have earlier read about "the course of this world" (Ephesians 2:2)—the course followed by "the children of disobedience." But being a Christian is going against that stream, against the course of the world in which success is measured by financial, social, or intellectual achievement. Over against that course of the world is the new life that the epistle promises: a life of love and service.

It is not easy to go against the stream. There is an old Spanish saying: "A shrimp that goes to sleep is carried away by the stream." A Christian who goes to sleep is carried away by the course of the world. It is necessary to stay awake. It is necessary to be strengthened by the Spirit (Ephesians 3:10). We must be constantly aware of the contrast between the "course of the world," which is part of that death of which Ephesians speaks, and the new life in Christ. It is not possible to enjoy that new life and at the same time let oneself be carried away by that course. A choice must be made. To decide for Christ is not simply a matter of raising your hand or responding to an altar call. It is above all being rid of the old life, which in truth is death, and living a new life.

Do you know someone who clearly lives in opposition to "the course of the world"? Do you admire that person? Why?

Act: Review what you have written in your notebook during this week regarding "the course of this world" and how to avoid following it. Ask for forgiveness in those cases when that course has carried you away, and ask for new strength to resist it. If at some point you have indeed resisted it, thank God for it, for this was God's work rather than yours. Write a prayer expressing these feelings. Repeat it.

Fifth Day: Read Ephesians 2:11-12.

See: This text requires some explanation. We have seen repeatedly that according to Ephesians all humans are children of disobedience, dead in our sins. Today the passage says that some were far away, thus implying that others were closer. In order to understand this, it is important to realize that Paul here is dealing with the relationship between Jews and Christians. As we read Paul's letters—particularly Romans and Galatians—we immediately note that this relationship was a serious problem.

What was the relationship between Christianity and Judaism? Clearly, at the beginning all Christians were Jews, as was Jesus himself and also all his apostles. Slowly, however, the church became increasingly Gentile and less Jewish. In these three verses Paul is beginning a section in which he tells Gentile Christians that they are just as valuable and just as acceptable before God as are their Jewish sisters and brothers.

Judge: The study of these three verses as well as those that follow provides a good opportunity to think about the relationship between Christianity and Judaism, and especially between followers of these two religions. This relationship is of paramount importance, for a serious misunderstanding of what the New Testament has to say about Judaism has led many Christians to be prejudiced against Jews and at times this has resulted in the slaughter of Jews. The New Testament does not say that Judaism is false or that Jews are evil or that their God is false. On the contrary, the New Testament confirms what the entire Bible says: that Jews were chosen by God as a people to receive God's revelation.

What has happened in Jesus Christ is that the revelation that the Jews had received has become available to Gentiles, and that Gentiles can now declare themselves also to be heirs of the history of God's dealings with Israel. This is the meaning of today's text: some were far away (Gentiles), and some were near (Jews). Yet in Christ we have been made one. We are no longer the alien latecomers. We are now children of Abraham, jointly with those who are his descendants according to the flesh.

This is what the text says, not that God has rejected the Jews. On the contrary, through God's grace, those of us who are of Gentile origin, who "were at that time without Christ, being aliens from the commonwealth of Israel, and strangers to the covenants of promise, having no hope and without God in the world," have now been brought near.

Act: Think of the Jews you know. Do you deal with them in love, as the children of God that they are? Are you grateful for all that God has done through Abraham and Sarah and their descendants? Remember, among other things, that it was through the Jewish people that we have received most of the Bible, and it was among that people, and as one of them, that Jesus came to us. Reflect on your relationship with Jews and how you can show them a love that reflects God's love for you. Write down your reflections and experiences.

Sixth Day: Read Ephesians 2:13-16.

See: We are still on the theme of the relationship of Jews and Christians. These verses speak of the enmity and the wall of separation between Jews and Gentiles. Paul refers to that wall of separation when he declares that Christ "has abolished the law with its commandments and ordinances that he might create in himself one humanity in place of the two, thus making peace." The commandments to which he refers, such as circumcision and the dietary laws, were the main wall of separation between Jews and Gentiles. But now Christ has broken down this dividing wall.

However, by extension, these verses also refer to all the various barriers that present-day Christians build to separate ourselves from one another. Such barriers have no place in a community that claims that Christ has brought down the dividing wall.

Note that unity has been bought at a high price. It is "in his flesh" and by his blood that we have been brought close to one another. The walls of separation must then be a powerful and evil reality, if Christ went to the cross to in order to tear them down.

Judge: What barriers are there within your church or faith community? Sometimes we disagree about what the church ought or ought not to do. There is nothing wrong with such disagreements, for it is out of a diversity of opinions that the best ideas are born. But if we allow those disagreements to become divisions, full of bickering or jealousy, this may well be a grave sin. If Christ died on the cross in order to tear down the dividing wall, and yet we build new walls, are we not saying that Christ died in vain?

What kind of witness can Christians give to a divided world if we ourselves are divided? If we allow divisions to continue existing among us, is it not possible that we are simply being carried away by "the course of this world"?

Act: If you have grown apart from some people in your church, make a list of their names. Next to the name of each person, write down the reasons for your distance. Do this as sincerely as you can, knowing that your notebook is a private matter.

After having completed this task, review the names one at a time. Ask yourself in each particular case, *Are the reasons that I have given sufficiently important that I am justified in trying to rebuild the dividing wall that Christ has torn down?* Write down your reflections. If time allows, repeat this exercise, this time listing not names of people but rather of churches or denominations that rival yours. Can we continue justifying our divisions once we have received the message of the cross of Christ, who through his flesh and with his blood has destroyed all hostility?

Seventh Day: Read Ephesians 2:17-22.

See: According to Paul, the Jewish people were called by God, who gave them their laws and commandments. One of these laws is about circumcision, which God did command to be performed. But this does not mean that in order to become Christians, Gentiles have to become Jews.

The Jews are those who according to verse 17 "were near." The Gentiles are those who "were far off." The entire epistle to the Ephesians, and therefore today's passage, is directed mostly to Gentile believers. They are the ones whom Paul calls "you Gentiles by birth." What Paul tells these believers is that they are "no longer strangers and aliens." They are not second-class believers because they were not Jewish. Nor do they have to be circumcised and practice all the Jewish rites. Christ has destroyed the ancient division between Jews and Gentiles and has created "one new humanity in place of the two."

Note that, according to verse 18, both Jews and Gentiles have access to the Father by the Spirit. Paul does not speak as if the Jews had one way of access and now Gentiles who join the church have a different way. Neither of the two groups has an advantage.

The result is that now both groups are "members of the household of God." In other words, believers both of Jewish and Gentile origin are now part not only of the same people, but even of the same family. They are kindred, even though they cannot point to a common lineage. Now Jews and Gentiles are built together as if they were a holy temple. Here they all have a part, for they are built "spiritually into a dwelling place for God."

Judge: The text speaks of a people who were near and another who were far and declares that, in Christ, those who were far are no longer strangers but are members of the same people, with the same citizenship, in the same family.

As a Latino Protestant, in reading this text I immediately think of the relationship of Latinos with Christians in the dominant culture. Protestantism came to us from that culture. In that sense, we (or our ancestors) were far. Our ancestors were not part of the churches to which we now belong. Our church heritage we have received mostly from an English-speaking culture, just as the first Gentile Christians received their faith from Jewish Christians. For this reason, it is relatively easy for Hispanic Protestants to consider ourselves "far" and those of the dominant culture "near."

But the passage applies also to those of the dominant culture. Given the history of the last few centuries, it is easy for them to think that they have always been "near" and that it is people from other cultures and other lands who are "far," or who have been brought in after being "far."

Neither of these two positions fully reflects what Paul is saying. Remember our earlier discussions about being brought to life out of death. In that sense, we were all "far." What makes us "near" is nothing but the grace of God, who makes no distinctions between cultures or races, between natives and strangers. According to the passage we are studying, in this new people that God has created there are "no longer strangers and aliens," for we all hold equal citizenship with the saints and are all members of the same family.

The image at the end of our passage, of the church as a building, Christ being the cornerstone, shows this clearly. In a building, every stone has a place. Those that were brought into the building earlier are not necessarily more important than those that came later. Furthermore, each stone is important, not by itself but as part of the building. In Christ we are a single building. As isolated stones, we are not much; our true worth is in being part of the building. And this is equally true of the very first stones to be placed and of the ones that have just recently been added to the structure.

Act: Try to think in two directions at the same time. These two ideas may seem opposed to each other, but in truth they lead to the same conclusion. First, remember that if you are a believer you are such only by the grace of Christ, and the same is true of every other person, no matter how seemingly important or holy. There is no church leader, be it in our land and culture or in any other culture or time, who actually deserves anything. Therefore, no one is worth more than you are. Think about this and write down your conclusions. But then, remember that Christ died for you and for everybody else whom you may meet along the paths of life. This means that you, as well as those other people, are of great worth. If others humiliate you, they are demeaning Christ and his cross. And the same is true if you denigrate another. Write down your reflections on this score.

For Group Study

Tell the group the following true story: In one of our cities there were two congregations sharing the same facilities. One of them, by far older and richer but also much smaller, belonged to the dominant race and culture. The other, much more recent and poorer but with many more members and activities, was a minority church. At some point the conflicts between the two groups came to such a point that the bishop had to intervene.

In his visit, after listening to what each group had to say, the bishop addressed the minority group, saying: "Remember that, after all, you are guests here. You must behave as such."

Now lead the group in a discussion of this story, and in particular of the bishop's words. To whom does the church belong? Who is the host? Who are the guests? (We may well say that the real host is Jesus Christ. It is clearly wrong to think that the church belongs to some believers, and that the rest are guests or visitors.) At the end of the discussion, read the Bible passage again, and ask the group what they think Paul would have said about this situation. If time permits, have them write in Paul's name to this congregation, using as many phrases and ideas from Ephesians as they can.

W E E K

TEN

First Day: Read Ephesians 3:1.

See: Note that the reason that Paul gives for his imprisonment is what we saw last week. This new chapter begins precisely with the words "This is the reason." Oddly enough, Paul has just declared that the work of Jesus is one of reconciliation; but now it turns out that this word of reconciliation has brought him to jail.

To understand this it may be well to look at Acts 21. There we are told that Paul was arrested because some among the Jewish leadership disliked his preaching to the Gentiles. It was they who accused him before the Romans. Therefore, although Paul finds himself in a Roman prison, most likely in Rome itself, the reason for this is that he took very seriously what he has just told us in chapter 2. His message of reconciliation between Jew and Gentile was not well received by some of the Jewish leadership in Jerusalem, and this has brought him to prison.

Now we understand why Paul says he is in prison "for the sake of you Gentiles." Paul is in prison for having invited Gentiles to join the people of God without following the whole process of conversion to Judaism. He is in prison for having told Gentiles that the ancient promises made to Abraham and his descendants are now available to them.

Judge: It may seem strange at first that Paul is in prison for having preached reconciliation. But the truth is that reconciliation is not as easy as some might think. When there is prejudice and enmity, some people consider themselves superior to others.

Normally, people on both sides consider themselves superior to their opponents. Thus, those seeking a reconciliation must tell people on both sides that they are not superior. Quite commonly, this creates a negative reaction toward those proposing reconciliation. Paul earned the enmity of the Jewish leadership because, if what he was telling the Gentiles was true, Jews were not superior to Gentiles. This was something they could not tolerate.

This is why the cross of Christ stands at the center of the work of reconciliation. The cross itself is a sign that reconciliation is not easy, and that quite often it is achieved only at a high price.

Think about divisions or bitterness among people you know. Examine your own congregation to see if you know of such divisions within it. If you were to devote yourself to reconciliation, is it not likely that both sides would consider you an enemy?

Last week we were talking about the variety of cultures within the church. We must acknowledge that the variety of cultures and races within the church often leads to suspicion, prejudice, and even division. This is a sign that there is a need for reconciliation. There is need for a true reconciliation in which each contending group asks itself if it has sinned against the other, and both have made a commitment to be truly one in Christ. However, that very need for reconciliation may mean that any who seek peace and unity between contending groups will find themselves rejected by both. Once again, the work of reconciliation is not easy.

Act: Look around you to see where there may be a need for reconciliation. Pray for both sides and for unity between them. If you feel that God is calling you to do so, approach both sides and seek reconciliation. Do not be surprised, however, if you arouse the suspicion of both sides.

Second Day: Read Ephesians 3:2-7.

See: The epistle turns again to the theme of mystery. Paul claims that this mystery was given to him "by revelation." This might lead us to think that he is claiming a private revelation. But as we read on, we find that the mystery has been "revealed to his holy apostles and prophets by the Spirit." It is not then a private revelation to Paul, but rather a revelation given to the church by the Spirit to its leaders. Paul then explains the contents of this mystery, namely that "the Gentiles have become fellow heirs, members of the same body." Even though it does not use the word "mystery," the book of Acts speaks of this revelation. Remember, for instance, Peter's vision and the conversion of Cornelius. Through these events, the Spirit revealed to Peter and then to the whole church that "God has given even to the Gentiles the repentance that leads to life" (Acts 11:18).

Paul's words in verse 3 that he has written "in a few words," may be understood in various ways. The NRSV understands this phrase as referring to the earlier part of the epistle, and therefore says that Paul has written of these things "above." But others believe this to be a reference to a lost letter of Paul's, or perhaps to the epistle to the Laodiceans, which Paul had written so that it might circulate among the churches (Colossians 4:16).

Judge: The "mystery" Paul proclaims is that God's eternal design is one of inclusiveness. In the situation in which Paul is writing, this design refers particularly to the ancient division between Jews and Gentiles—between those who were descended from Abraham and Sarah and those who were not. Paul is referring to the barrier between these two when he says that Christ has torn down the "wall of division" (Ephesians 2:14).

For many of us today the most serious division is not that between Jew and Gentile. Instead, we have built other walls of division. Can you think of walls of division affecting your own life and the communities within which you live? Are there walls of division or of exclusion based on race, culture, national origin, education, social class, gender, or others? Are you a part of this process of division?

If Paul were writing to us today, what would he tell us about the mystery of unity and inclusiveness that God has revealed in Jesus Christ?

Act: Make a note in your notebook regarding any "walls of division" keeping you apart from others. Now think about each of them. To what extent are you the one who built the walls and still supports them, and to what extent do others do this?

Next to each of these walls, write your conclusion as to who has built the wall. For instance, write "I," or "they," or "both." Wherever you wrote "I" or "both," pray, asking for forgiveness for having excluded others. As soon as possible, ask them for forgiveness. Where you wrote "both," pray for forgiveness as well as for wisdom and strength to go across the wall and be reconciled with the other side. Wherever you wrote "they," take some time to make sure that this is the case, and that you are not simply blaming someone else for what was at least partly your fault. You will probably find that you will reclassify that item under either "both" or "I." Then proceed accordingly.

Third Day: Read Ephesians 3:8-9.

See: Paul now refers to his particular ministry among the Gentiles. He makes it clear that if he has received this ministry, it is not because of any particular merit on his part. On the contrary, he is "the very least of all the saints." Therefore, his task of bringing to the Gentiles "the news of the boundless riches of Christ" is a "grace"—that is, something that God has done. Remember that it is as a consequence of this grace of God that Paul is in prison. But in spite of this Paul holds that the task that has led him to his present situation is a favor from God.

In verse 9 the word "mystery" comes up again. Note that here, as before, this mystery has been "hidden for ages in God," and has now been revealed. Note also that this mystery refers to the absolute scope of the power and mercy of the God "who created all things."

Judge: Note the use of the words "all" and "everyone" in these two verses. (Remember that we saw this to be a central theme in Colossians.) Here Paul, while calling himself "the very least of all," announces the gospel of the God "who created all things."

Do you see a relationship between these two cases in which the word "all" appears—between Paul's being the least of all the saints and yet being called to proclaim the message of the God who created all things? Could it be that it is precisely when we feel important that we dare determine that some things fall outside God's power of redemption? If I am the least of all, I dare not tell others that they are less than I am. If, on the contrary, I imagine that because of my goodness or holiness God loves me and forgives me, I shall soon find someone who is less holy and therefore less worthy of love and forgiveness. When we in the church exclude some people, could it be that we are forgetting the grace of God, a grace so surprising that it includes even us?

Act: Pray: "God all-powerful and all-merciful, give me the humility to see that before you I am as nothing; that it was out of sheer grace that you loved me and forgave me; that I have no right to consider myself better than anyone else; that the mystery of your divine love, which includes one such as myself, can include anybody else. Help me see other people as your children and show them a glimpse of your love. In the name of Jesus Christ, your love made flesh. Amen."

Fourth Day: Read Ephesians 3:10.

See: This verse points to an aspect of the gospel and its consequences that we seldom remember. According to Paul, the preaching of the gospel has an impact beyond the people to whom we preach. Apparently, "the rulers and authorities in the heavenly places" did not know "the wisdom of God in its rich variety." Furthermore, this wisdom is made known to them through the preaching of the Gospel.

In order to begin to understand these words we must remember that "rulers" and "authorities" were names sometimes given to invisible beings. Later we shall see that Paul declares that our struggle is with them. It is impossible to know all that this means. But at least it is a hint that creation is much wider than we imagine. In the Bible there is repeated talk of spiritual beings that are not seen, such as angels, archangels, and demons. In some manner that we may not be able to understand, when Paul preaches to the Gentiles, the message of the rich variety of God's wisdom reaches also the rulers and principalities.

Judge: Are you surprised by this verse? I am not only surprised but also confounded. As people born, raised, and educated in the modern world, we have grown accustomed to thinking that there is in creation nothing more than what we see. But the truth is that even the strictest scientific experiment can never prove that this is so. This vision of creation, like many others, is simply something we take for granted because it is thus that we have learned to think. Yet, God's creation includes much more than what we see. It even includes much more than what our imaginations might conceive.

However, let us not use this verse as an excuse for claiming that now we know all there is to know. Some people take verses such as this and upon them build schemes listing the various kinds of celestial beings and how they relate among themselves. Here, only "rulers" and "authorities" are mentioned. Later on in this study we shall see that this is not an exhaustive list. Rather than trying to find out how many sorts of such beings there are, and classifying them as if they were fish in a pond or plants in a garden, what we are to do is to marvel before the inscrutable greatness and complexity of God's creation.

Does this verse confuse you as it does me? Is confusion always bad? Or are there cases in which the most we can do is simply accept our confusion as a reminder that "the wisdom of God in its rich variety" is infinitely greater than our own wisdom?

Were we able to explain and classify all of creation, from the least subatomic particle to the highest celestial beings, would this not mean that we were claiming a wisdom as great as God's? Is there not in this verse a reminder of the gulf between God's wisdom and ours?

Act: Pray: "I thank you, immeasurably wise God, that your creation is so much richer than anything I could imagine. I thank you that a God as great as you, who created atoms and electrons, stars and planets, rulers and principalities, has loved even me, small as I am. Teach me to love and praise your mystery, the rich variety of your wisdom, your knowledge so high that I cannot comprehend it. Amen."

Fifth Day: Ephesians 3:11-12.

See: Paul turns again to the "eternal purpose" of God. Remember that the "mystery" has been hidden from all ages. What God is now doing in Paul is not something at the last minute; it is part of God's eternal purpose. This is closely related to what verse 12 says about boldness and confidence. When we think of God's immensity, and especially when, as we did yesterday, we stand in awe before the rich variety of God's wisdom, there is always the possibility of becoming fearful and doubting. If God is so great compared to human smallness, who is Paul that he dares be bold and confident? If God's action is so mysterious, how can Paul trust it? The answer, though simple, is profound: Paul can trust God and God's action because God's action is part of God's eternal purpose. If God is great, so is God's purpose. Therefore, Paul declares that faith allows us to have confidence and boldness in approaching God, even though God is so much greater than we.

Judge: Yesterday we concluded our study stressing the great wisdom of God, shown in a creation so marvelous that we cannot even encompass all of it. Our mood was like that of the Psalmist (Psalm 139:6):

> Such knowledge is too wonderful for me;
>   it is so high that I cannot attain it.

It is important for us to retain this attitude, for sometimes we believe in a God so small as to be able to do only what we are able to understand.

However, when we think of God in such grand, far-reaching terms, there is always the danger that we may be overcome by fear and despair. If God is so great, who am I before such immensity? If God has created not only this earth with all its beauty and complexity, and not only the most distant stars, constellations, and galaxies, but also the mysterious beings that Paul calls "powers" and "authorities," who am I to presume that God cares about me?

Here lies the importance of Paul's declaration that his life and ministry are part of God's eternal creation. God is certainly great; but that greatness includes the least of us in its eternal purpose. This is why, although God is powerful beyond all imagination, we may still approach the heavenly throne with confidence and boldness.

Have you ever experienced this sense of purpose?

Act: Pray: "My God, yesterday I praised you for your power, for your inscrutable mysteries. Today I praise you even more because in your greatness and inscrutable mystery you have included even me in your eternal purpose. Make me obedient to that purpose. Give me confidence and boldness in approaching you, so that I may face all the challenges of life with equal confidence and boldness. Amen."

Sixth Day: Read Ephesians 3:13.

See: The word "therefore" indicates that what follows is a consequence of what has been said before. In other words, what Paul is now about to say is based on what he has just said. And what he is going to tell them is that they should "not lose heart over my sufferings for you." Apparently, Paul is concerned that these believers, upon hearing of his imprisonment, will be discouraged. Remember that this study began with Paul writing to the Philippians from prison a letter overflowing with joy. It is difficult to be enthusiastic when things are not going as we would like. But Paul tells his readers that his being in prison should not discourage them.

How are they not to be discouraged? From where will they draw strength? Precisely from what Paul has just told them, namely, that Paul's ministry (and therefore also the faith of his readers) is part of God's eternal purpose. Even though Paul is imprisoned, they are not to lose heart, for the one who guides him is the God who has created all things, the God of wisdom in all its variety, the God whose eternal purpose is of love for all creation. Paul tells them more: His own sufferings are the "glory" of his readers. Why? For the same reason: because such sufferings are a sign that God loves them so as to give them someone such as Paul, who even while in prison remembers them and tells them not to lose heart.

Judge: Do you know congregations who seem to have lost heart and have no enthusiasm left? In such churches people sing as if their praise would not rise above the ceiling. People pray as if no response were expected. Preaching becomes a matter of filling a few minutes with sound. There is constant talk of better times, when the neighborhood was different, when the church was more lively, or when there were fewer difficulties.

Sometimes people refer to such congregations as "dead." Is that the real problem? Or is it actually that they have forgotten that their ministry and their life are part of God's eternal purpose, and that therefore both their successes and their failings are in God's hands?

If we truly believe what Paul has been telling us throughout this week, do you think we should become discouraged to the point of having no joy or hope? Could it be that when a congregation seems to die what is actually dying is its faith and its vision of the enormous, surprising love of God?

Act: If there are in your congregation or faith community signs of such "death," make a list of the things that have made you and others lose heart. Pray that God will help you see all these things as someone who really trusts God's eternal purpose. Speak to others. Discuss how what has happened, or even what they fear, may be used to serve that eternal purpose.

If you are the one who tends to be dismayed before difficulties, do two things: Pray as frequently as possible, placing your difficulties and doubts in God's hands and asking for faith and strength to move on. Seek a group of people whom you trust and with whom you can share your doubts and hesitations. Offer to do the same for others in the group.

Seventh Day: Read Ephesians 3:14-21.

See: Note that what Paul says here is that he is doing precisely what was suggested that you do at the end of yesterday's study. He prays that his readers may be strengthened so that they will not lose heart. He prays "before the Father, from whom every family in heaven and on earth takes its name." The word "every" is important here, as it is throughout this epistle and in Colossians. That the name of "every family" comes from God means that Jews as well as Gentiles are part of God's creation and eternal purpose. In saying "every family," Paul is reiterating his earlier assertion that the mystery of God's will is to bring together all things in Christ.

It is to this great God, Lord of "every family," that Paul prays, asking strength for his readers. He asks precisely that they be not dismayed, that they not be disheartened by the news of his imprisonment or by any other difficulty. This is the meaning of his prayer, that they "may be strengthened in your inner being with power through his Spirit." If they are "being rooted and grounded in love," Christ will dwell in their hearts through faith.

Note that throughout this section of the epistle Paul is giving his readers the necessary tools so that they will not be dismayed or grow disheartened by difficulties.

It is within this context that we find the well-known lines regarding the love of Christ: "that you may have the power to comprehend, with all the saints, what is the breadth and length and height and depth, and to know the love of Christ that surpasses knowledge." These words are so well known and so inspiring that we often repeat them without knowing what we are really saying. As we study them there are two points to be made.

First, note that Paul measures love in four dimensions rather than three. If someone asks us what is the size of a box or refrigerator, we respond by giving measurements in height, width, and depth. But if we imagine we are *inside* a building that is several stories high, we say that the building has a certain width, and a certain length, but also a certain height (above us) and a certain depth (below us). If we are, for instance, in the ground floor of a building, we say that the building is three hundred feet by two hundred, with four stories above us and two stories in the basement below. In other words, when we are *inside* what we measure, we often speak of four measurements instead of three. Likewise, Paul is looking at the love of Christ not from the outside, like someone measuring a box or a refrigerator, but rather as someone who is submerged in the love of Christ, surrounded by that love on all sides—as when we are within a building. He therefore speaks of breadth and length and height and depth. (Note that just before these words, Paul has declared that his readers are "rooted and grounded in love," that is, that they are within that love to whose dimensions he now refers.)

The second point to be noted in this passage, as elsewhere in the epistles we are studying, is the frequency of various words indicating totality, particularly in reference to "all the saints," and "all the fullness of God." Paul does not call them to have more knowledge of, or to believe in a greater God, but rather to have the fullness of the love of God.

Joining these two points, we see that Paul is saying that the love of Christ is so great, and we are so submerged in it, that it is impossible for us to leave it. It is as if we were within a building so high, with such a deep basement and such a great expanse, that no matter how much we climb or descend or move from one place to another, we will still be in it. It is the full knowledge of that peerless love that allows Paul's readers not to lose heart.

Finally, now that the epistle is coming to the end of its doctrinal section, Paul comes back to a doxology similar to the one we saw in the first chapter: "Now to him who by the power at work within us ... to him be glory...." In this doxology we see once more that Paul is grounding his words of encouragement on God's power. The important point here is that God "is able to accomplish abundantly far more than all we can ask or imagine."

Judge: What do you think would happen if the church really believed what Paul says here? Do you think we would have the same problems? Do you think we would lose heart when things do not turn out as we would like? What would happen to the petty divisions and squabbles among us?

Look at the same matter from the opposite angle: If we lose heart, could it be that we have not understood the immensity of the love that enwraps us? If we bicker over unimportant matters, could it be that we imagine that God's love depends on the decisions the church takes? If we judge one another harshly, could it be that we think that God's loving us depends on what we do or don't do?

If the love of Christ is as great as Paul declares, could it be that all those people whom we consider to be far away from God, sinners without any apparent possibility of redemption, are still within the scope of that love, even if they themselves do not know it? If the love of Christ is so wide, so long, so high, and so deep, can we not feel free to go to the worst places on earth, knowing that even there we are surrounded by God's love?

Act: A few days ago you were invited to think of some people who seemed to be far away from God and to resolve to approach them. Did you? On the basis of what we have just studied, you should know that as you approach these people, Christ is there far ahead of you. Approach them again, remembering that both you and they are enveloped in Christ's love. (If this helps, you may think in terms of the building mentioned above. Both you and these other people are in the same building even though they do not know it. Upon approaching them, you are not leaving the building. You are simply discovering that it is much larger than you thought.)

Review what you wrote about people who were separated from you by walls of division. In the light of what we have just studied, resolve to approach them again and again and again— until the love of Christ triumphs.

For Group Study

You may begin today's session by reviewing what we have studied during the week. Above all, make sure that the group sees the relationship between the mystery of God's eternal purpose of including *all* and the certainty that believers are to have. Connect this to what Paul says about his own imprisonment and how his readers are not to lose heart. Then move on to today's study, stressing how the certainty of the love of Christ helps us not to lose heart.

In order to explain the four dimensions of the love of Christ that Paul mentions, you may draw a building of several stories, including a deep basement, with a person inside. Explain that in the case of the love to which Paul refers, this building is as large as all of creation.

W E E K

ELEVEN

First Day: Read Ephesians 4:1-3.

See: The last two chapters of Ephesians turn to what seem to be more practical matters. This was part of the typical structure of letters at the time: one began with the names of the author and the addressees, gave a greeting, invoked the gods, and then turned to general matters. Toward the end of the letter one would turn to more concrete issues, often based on what had been said before. At the end there was a series of greetings.

Ephesians follows this structure, except that, instead of invoking the gods, it praises the God and Father of our Lord Jesus Christ. At this point, the beginning of chapter 4, we turn to more concrete matters, although all of them are grounded on the first three chapters.

Given the tone of the entire letter, it is not surprising that the first piece of advice is to maintain unity. Paul calls his readers to bear "with one another in love, making every effort to maintain the unity of the Spirit in the bond of peace." Apparently in order to make his advice more authoritative, Paul reminds them that he is a "prisoner in the Lord." Thus, the one calling them to live in the bond of peace is himself living in a different sort of bondage.

Judge: Why do you think that in a passage such as this, calling his readers to unity, Paul also calls them to patience? Could it be that the two are related?

Think of an occasion on which your congregation has been divided. If both parties had exercised greater patience, would the division have been avoided? Would patience have made it possible to reach an agreement?

The same happens between neighbors. If there is no patience, neighbors end up hating each other because one's dog barks at midnight, or because someone parks in the wrong place, or because the children of one break the window of the other, or for any other of a thousand possible reasons. But ultimately the true reason is that there is no patience.

How about you? Have you been lacking in patience with someone? Would your relationship have been better with a bit more patience?

Act: Pray: "Lord, your patience with me has been manifold. So often have I abandoned your ways—and then I have done it again and again! But your patient love has brought me back. Help me show others a patience that reflects yours, so that we may keep unity and give the world a witness worthy of the love with which you have loved us. In Jesus Christ, your patient love made flesh. Amen."

Second Day: Read Ephesians 4:4-7.

See: Note that the passage may be divided into three parts or steps, and that in each of them a word stands out indicating number: (1) From verse 4 to the middle of verse 6, the dominant word is *one*. (2) In the rest of verse 6, the dominant word is *all*. (3) Finally, in verse 7, we turn to *each*.

All of these words are closely wound together. It is precisely because there is "one Lord, one faith, one baptism, one God and Father" that this God is "Father of all, who is above all and through all and in all." If there were two lords or two gods, neither of the two would be the God and Father of all. It is precisely because there is only one God that it is possible to speak of "all," as this passage and the entire epistle to the Colossians do.

It is within that universal power of God that "each one of us" has our place. We are certainly different, but this is not because we have different gods or because we have different baptisms or a different faith. The difference is that God has given out different gifts. We shall see more of this the day after tomorrow.

For the time being, what is important is to remember that the unity among Christians is based on the singleness of God who is Father of all and is over all.

Judge: When in your congregation there is talk about other believers, does the emphasis fall on the bond of unity among all believers in Christ? Or is the emphasis rather on the differences, as if those others were not true believers? There certainly may be doctrinal differences; yet do you believe that essentially the faith, hope, and baptism of all Christians are one? Or do you think that only those who believe as you do and baptize exactly as your church does are true believers?

What would Paul say about the ease with which churches break apart today, sometimes over minor doctrinal issues, and often even over the personalities of their leaders?

Act: Resolve that during the coming week you will approach someone belonging to another church. You are not to do this in order to bring that other person to your church, but rather that each of you may understand and appreciate the other's faith and so that together you may be able to experience that unity of which Paul speaks.

Third Day: Read Ephesians 4:8-10.

See: At first sight it is difficult to see why Paul places these verses in the middle of a passage on the unity of the church and the diversity of gifts. The reason seems to be the need for his readers to understand that the gifts come from Christ, the only Lord of the church.

At any rate, the passage is important because it leads us to think of the work of Christ in ways that are not the most common but are very important. The quotation is from Psalm 68:18, a passage in which Israel sings the victory of its God. Here, Paul applies the same words to the victory of Jesus over the powers of evil. Jesus descended to earth and died, but in his resurrection and ascension he "made captivity itself a captive." This means that he showed himself to be the conqueror over sin and over the powers of evil that had held us captive.

Among early Christian writers, it was commonly said that in his death and resurrection Christ "killed death"—in other words, that what Jesus has done for us is to achieve a great victory over the powers that held us in bondage, thus making it possible for us to be free children of God. It is this Lord, conqueror of evil, who made captivity captive, and who gave the gifts to which we shall turn tomorrow.

Judge: Quite often we hear a lot about Jesus as a sacrificial victim who suffered in our stead. It is important not to forget that. But here we find another image of Jesus that is equally important: Jesus as the conqueror over death, who led captivity captive. What significance do you see in these two ways of understanding the work of Jesus? For instance, could it be that if we always think of Jesus as a victim, and never as a victor, our faith will be less joyous, less victorious? Were we to think of Jesus as the conqueror over death, sin, and the powers of evil, how would this affect our actions and our thoughts?

Act: Pray: "Thank you, my God and God of the church, that you sent your Son to die and suffer for us. Thank you that, through his death, we live. Thank you because, after his death on the cross, you made him a victor over death. And thank you because, in his victory, you have also made us victorious. Make us more than conquerors through faith in the One who conquered the tomb and led captivity captive. Amen."

Fourth Day: Read Ephesians 4:11-12.

See: Two days ago we noted that the one God has given grace to "each one." Today we see that grace being manifested in a variety of gifts, so that some are "prophets" (which then meant people who preached and expounded the will of God to the church), others "evangelists," others "apostles," and others "teachers."

It is important to understand that this is not an exhaustive list of all the gifts believers may receive. Remember that Paul had said that "each of us was given grace according to the measure of Christ's gift." This means that all Christians receive gifts. The list in verse 11 does not include everyone. Also, in other letters Paul offers similar but not identical lists. Therefore, what we have here are some examples of the way in which gifts work, not an exhaustive list of all gifts.

Then, and probably even more important, we must note that the gifts are given not for the benefit of those who receive them, but rather "for the work of ministry, for building up the body of Christ." The gifts that each of us receives are not really for ourselves, but rather for the building up of the entire body.

Judge: Have you seen cases in which divisions have appeared in the church because everyone wished to employ their gifts in their own fashion? Imagine the chaos if in a church there were a young man with a beautiful voice, a woman who played the piano, and a man who played the flute. But instead of their using these gifts in order to produce the same music, the young man sings in his own rhythm, while the other two people play in different keys. The result, rather than harmonious music, would be jarring noise. This is what happens when we each want to use our gifts in our own fashion, forgetting that they have been given, not that we might shine, but for the building up of the entire body of Christ.

Act: In response to your study of this passage, do the following two things:

First, consider the gifts you have received and how you may employ them for the building up of the entire body. Think not only of the gifts that sound "religious," but of all your gifts. For instance, if you have the gift of making money, how would you use it for the building up of the body of Christ? Or if you have the gift of teaching, how would you use it for the same purpose? Write down your reflections and decisions.

Second, think of others whose gifts you know. What can you do to help them discover those gifts and use them for the building up of the whole body? Resolve to speak to them about the matter. Once again, write down your reflections.

Fifth Day: Read Ephesians 4:13-16.

See: The goal of all the preceding, what we have been studying in the last few days, is that "all of us come to the unity of the faith and of the knowledge of the Son of God, to maturity, to the measure of the full stature of Christ." When we read the words "all of us," we may understand them in one of two ways: they could mean each on his or her own, or they could mean all together. For instance, if we say "all" the players on a team are at least six feet tall, we are referring to them individually. But if we say that "all" of them together are a great team, we are referring to them as a whole, and not individually.

The Greek language makes it clear that in today's passage Paul is speaking not of every individual reaching the goal, but rather all together, as a single reality, as a single body, reaching the goal that is here described. This is why that goal is described not in the plural, but in the singular: "the measure of the full stature of Christ." The goal is that *all together* will be one body, perfect and united, so that we will no longer be "tossed to and fro and blown about by every wind of doctrine" but will be a "whole body, joined and knit together by every ligament with which it is equipped." The result will be the growth of the entire body.

Judge: There has been much talk in the church about Christian perfection. Almost always when people speak of perfection, what they mean is the individual perfection of believers. However, in this image the "full stature" of perfection is a matter not for individual members, but rather for the entire body of Christ.

Do you believe it is possible to reach Christian maturity individually, without the entire body of the faithful attaining such maturity? Could it be that when each of us seeks perfection on our own, we actually endanger the unity without which perfection is impossible?

Act: Pray for perfection, but not for your own individual perfection. Pray rather for the perfection of the church. Pray concretely that in your own congregation there will be such unity that all together may be able to "come to the unity of the faith and of the knowledge of the Son of God, to maturity, to the measure of the full stature of Christ." Pray, asking that the various gifts in your congregation will become so intertwined that those who have them will be like a single body joined by healthy ligaments.

Sixth Day: Read Ephesians 4:17-24.

See: We are in the section where the epistle draws out the practical implications of the doctrines discussed in the earlier part of the letter.

The text begins by telling its readers that they "must no longer live as the Gentiles live." We have noted that in the earlier part of the epistle there was much said about the relationship between Gentile and Jewish Christians (between the *we* of Paul and other Jewish Christians and the *you* of the Gentile Christians). The letter declares that in Christ both groups are one, for Christ has torn down the wall of division.

Those who are descendants of Abraham and Sarah according to the flesh have no advantage over those who have recently joined the people of God through the cross of Christ. But this does not mean that they are to go on living as the Gentiles do. There is nothing wrong with being a Christian of Gentile origin, but such Christians must not follow the typical behavior of the Gentiles as described in verses 18 and 19.

In contrast, those who have learned about Christ must be clothed in a new self. They are to be covered in "true righteousness and holiness." (This may refer to baptism, for in ancient times it was customary upon leaving the baptismal waters to receive a new, white garment, as a sign of newness of life.)

Judge: In early Christianity, when there was a marked contrast between Christian practices and those that were common in society, it was not difficult to distinguish between Christians and the rest. First of all, the Gentiles had a multitude of gods, while the church insisted that there was only one God, creator and sustainer of all that exists. In their practical life the contrasts were even greater. For instance, Christian faith insisted on the sanctity of life and the need to protect it; but among the Gentiles it was customary, if a father did not wish to raise a newborn son (or, as was usually the case, a daughter), simply to abandon the baby to the elements and the beasts.

Today the contrast is not as clear. Much of what the church taught in the beginning has now become common practice in the surrounding society. In many aspects, the church also is less strict than it used to be.

Given these situations, what would be today's equivalent to putting away our old self and being clothed with the new? What are we called to leave behind? How are Christians to be distinguished from the rest?

Act: Write down your answers to these questions. Read them slowly, asking yourself: Is this what I do? Do I act as I think people of faith should?

Pray, asking for forgiveness for your sins and shortcomings, and asking God to help you be clothed with a new self in Christ so that the world may believe.

Seventh Day: Read Ephesians 4:25-32.

See: The epistle now turns to more concrete practices, both positive and negative. The passage is essentially about things one ought to do and other things one ought not to do. Although this section is a list of moral practices, it is important to point out that they are generally based on what has been said earlier in the letter. Moral virtues have a theological foundation.

This is seen clearly in verse 25, which deals with the need to put away falsehood and embrace truth. The reason is that "we are members one of another." A body cannot subsist if there is not truthful communication among its members.

Imagine a body in which the eyes deceive the feet. It would be impossible for such a body to walk without stumbling and falling. Or imagine a body in which when there is a problem the member that suffers does not let the rest of the body know. Such a body will soon die, for it will have no means to respond to disease. This is what actually happens in the body of Christ if its members do not communicate truthfully among themselves. The body will not work properly. It cannot walk as it ought. It cannot respond to disease. Every untruth within the body of Christ weakens it, just as miscommunication within our own physical body weakens it.

Verse 26 is quite realistic. Anger is not forbidden. What is forbidden is to allow anger to lead us to sin. It is also forbidden to feed such anger to the point that it continues day after day: "Do not let the sun go down on your anger." As the next verse says, nurturing anger makes "room for the devil."

Verse 28 commends work. Note, however, that the purpose of work is not to become rich, but rather to be able to share with the needy.

Bad language is to be avoided, for it does not build up the body nor does it "give grace to those who hear." Finally, verses 30-32 present a list of attitudes to be avoided and others to be embraced, so as not to "grieve the Holy Spirit of God."

Judge: We often imagine that the main reason we are to behave in a particular way is to cultivate our own holiness and purity. That is certainly important, but note that throughout this passage what is to guide the behavior of believers is their concern over the well-being of the whole body and not grieving the Spirit. In other words, the real foundation for Christian morality is not personal purity, but love for others and for God.

Read the passage anew, noting this important point. Untruth is evil, not merely because those who speak it are stained by it, but also and above all because it damages the body of Christ. Work is good, not only because it is dignified and gives us a sense of accomplishment, but also because through it we obtain resources to share. Sins are to be avoided because they grieve the Holy Spirit. And the reason we are to forgive one another is because Christ forgave us.

Do you think that this way of understanding Christian behavior is better than when we think in purely individualistic terms, as if only *my* purity mattered?

Act: Divide a sheet in your notebook into two columns. Read the text slowly, writing in the lefthand column the evil things that the text urges us to avoid, and in the righthand column those we ought to pursue.

After completing the list, consider how those in the lefthand column weaken the body of Christ. Think concretely in terms of the congregation to which you belong. Try to remember what you or others have done that have weakened the body of Christ.

Now try to decide which of these things most commonly tempts you and how it affects the body of Christ. Draw a circle around it so as not to forget it. Close your study session, asking God to help you be clothed in the new self, particularly in regard to what you have circled.

For Group Study

Lead the group in a discussion about how each of the negative things mentioned in the biblical text affects the body of Christ. Then ask what would be ways of avoiding or counteracting them.

W E E K
TWELVE

First Day: Read Ephesians 5:1-2.

See: As we studied last week, the new life Christ gives takes place in a new community of faith, which is the body of Christ. But this new life is also shown in new behavior. Those who have died to the old life are no longer to live by the old standards, but by the new.

Note that Paul bases his guidelines for behavior on what God has done for us. Christian behavior is not only a matter of being decent, or of obeying certain rules. It is rather a matter of being "imitators of God" (5:1) and living with a love similar to that of Christ, who "gave himself up for us" (5:2). Because God gave us life when we were dead, and because Christ loved us and gave himself up for us, we are to walk "as is proper among saints" (5:3).

Remember that the core of Christian faith is not outward behavior, but the new life that Christ gives us by virtue of his death and resurrection. Even so, new behavior is also important. Today's passage says it clearly: We are to imitate God and God's love. This means that all that is destructive, all that is unjust, all that is spiteful must be left behind as part of the old life to which we are dead.

Judge: Here the epistle sets its sights quite high. We are to be no less than "imitators of God." This sounds overwhelming until we remember that according to Genesis we have been made after the image of God. Therefore, when we seek to imitate God we are not setting before us an impossible goal, but rather being

—— 148 ——

true to that for which we were created. We are to imitate the God after whose image we were made.

In what are we to imitate God? Note that in this passage there is no mention of power or rule, but rather of self-giving. The God we imitate is the one who in Christ "gave himself up for us." Imitating God is not claiming omniscience or omnipotence; it is giving ourselves as Christ gave himself.

However, too often in our society this giving up of oneself is used to convince the weak that they must allow themselves to be exploited. Some girls are taught that their task in life is to serve men—their father, their brothers, and eventually their husband. Against such notions, it is important to stress that to give oneself in imitation of God is to give oneself with dignity and freedom. It is not to do something because society expects it of us. It is to give oneself as someone who bears the image of God, and who therefore must seek ways to serve without allowing exploitation.

Act: Review your actions during the past week. Can you remember cases when you acted out of self-interest rather than out of love? Consider how in such cases you could have been an imitator of the God who gave Godself for you. If, on the contrary, in your acts of service your dignity was trampled, remember that it is good to give oneself in imitation of God, but that in giving of oneself one must never forget that one bears the image of God. Consider then how you could have given of yourself while at the same time showing the dignity that is in you. (On this last point, remember that sometimes we serve others better by denying what they wish or expect, and thus opening the way for new understandings.)

Pray: "Teach me, Lord, to imitate you in my self-giving. And teach me also to remember that in my self-giving I bear your image. Amen."

Second Day: Read Ephesians 5:3-5.

See: Newness of life is manifested in various ways, but none is more important than newness of behavior. Throughout its history, the church has insisted that Christian life requires Christian behavior. Sometimes this insistence has gone overboard, leading people to think that one achieves a new life by behaving differently. As should be quite clear by now, this is not true. There is no way to earn a new birth. New birth results in new behavior, but new behavior does not result in new birth. A new life is a gift from God. It is from that gift that behavior follows.

These two verses offer a list of some of the main things that Christians must avoid. This includes fornication, impurity, and greed. But it also includes destructive speech. The text does not claim that any of these is worse than the other, although it does declare that greed is idolatry.

Judge: In the privacy of your study time, seek to measure your life in the light of this passage. Go one by one over the things mentioned. Do you practice any of them? Respond sincerely in your heart, in your privacy with God.

How has your conduct affected your Christian life? How has it affected your sharing in the body of Christ?

Act: Write down your reflections. If you wish, do so with just one or two words that you alone will be able to understand. Repeat the following prayer, first using the plural form and then the singular (for instance, the first time say "our God," and the second say "my God"):

"Thank you, our God, for the new life you have given us in Christ Jesus. Thank you, because we know that there is nothing we have done or anything we could have done to deserve it. Help us behave as behooves that life, as children of light and not of darkness. We pray in the name of Jesus Christ, our life and our light. Amen."

Third Day: Read Ephesians 5:6-8.

See: Verse 6 includes a theme that appeared already in verse 4, and will reappear later in verses 12 and 19. All these verses refer to words and to speech. There are words that destroy, and words that build. There are empty words and holy words.

One might think that, in comparison with what is said in the rest of the passage about fornication and impurity, the matter of words and speech is less important. But in fact, this passage deals as much with unholy words as with unholy actions.

In Scripture, words have power. Remember that God created by saying "Let there be." Remember also that the Gospel of John begins by telling us that Jesus is the Word of God. Words are important. What is true of the Word of God is also true, although obviously to a much lesser degree, of human speech.

Judge: Although we tend to think that words are only noise, the fact is that words and speech are an important part of behavior, for they not only show who we are, but also shape who we are.

Although we were told as children that "sticks and stones may break my bones but words will never harm me," this is not quite true. If a child is constantly told that he or she is bad, lazy, and worthless, the child is quite likely to become such. If, on the contrary, a child hears words of love, safety, and encouragement, the opposite effect will be achieved. Words are important. A lie told a thousand times is often accepted as truth. It might even function as the truth!

Human words have power to create what they say. If we speak evil of others, we produce evil. If we speak well, we create good. That is why this passage insists on the importance of words and speech.

Act: Resolve to avoid speaking ill of others. Resolve that at least for the rest of this week you will consciously seek to say something good and positive to everyone you meet. The results will surprise you. You may even decide that this is a good practice for the rest of your life!

Fourth Day: Read Ephesians 5:9-10.

See: Here we find a description of the "fruit of the light" that is parallel to but different from the list of the "fruit of the Spirit" in Galatians 5:22-23. There, the fruit of the Spirit is "love, joy, peace, patience, kindness, generosity, faithfulness, gentleness, and self-control." Here, the list is shorter: "all that is good and right and true." The very fact that these are similar but different tells us that in neither of them is Paul offering an exhaustive list. Both lists give us a way to recognize whether we have the Spirit or whether we live in the light by producing this sort of fruit.

Note further that these three elements in verse 9 are presented not as a list of various "fruits," but as a single fruit. It is not a matter of sometimes practicing goodness and at other times truth. It is rather that there is only one sort of action that is "good and right and true."

Judge: The joining of these three is important, for sometimes we would like to take one of them as if it were the most important and leave the others aside. There are some believers who are very good and kind but who are at a loss when they meet falsehood or injustice. Then there are others who are constantly defending what is right, but they do it with such acrimony that they lose the sense of goodness and sometimes exaggerate their points at the expense of truth. Finally, there are some Christians who are so concerned over every detail of doctrinal truth that they lose sight of what is good and right. None of this is the fruit of light that emerges from newness of life. The fruit of light is "all that is good and right and true," these three. And the three are so intertwined that one cannot exist without the others.

In our present Christian life, do we practice the three with equal strength and perseverance? Or is there one we must stress more in order to express the fullness of the fruit of light?

The same questions may be asked about our congregation. Is one of the three overemphasized at the expense of the others? Is one of them forgotten or set aside?

Act: Draw a triangle in your notebook. Write a word in each of the angles: the good, the right, the true. Take a moment to think about each of the corners of the triangle. Consider how it is possible so to center on a particular corner that the rest of the triangle is forgotten. (Think, for instance, of the Inquisitors, who were so concerned over true doctrine that they were ready to torture and kill those who did not accept it. They were convinced they were serving truth; but what they did was certainly neither good nor right.)

Now place yourself within the triangle. Toward which of the corners do you lean? Note that the closer you get to one of the corners the farther you move from the others. Pray, asking God to guide you so that you may do what is good, right, and true.

Fifth Day: Read Ephesians 5:11-17.

See: The subject is still the contrast between the old life and the new. This contrast is now expressed by the image of light and darkness that was introduced in verse 8: "For once you were darkness, but now in the Lord you are light." Evil is practiced in the darkness. But when the light comes everything is exposed.

This reminds us that when the final light shines, in the day when God illumines all, all our works, no matter how hidden they may have been in darkness, will be exposed. Therefore, walking in light is walking as those who know that in the end the light will overcome, and the evil that is done in darkness will be made manifest.

Verse 14 presents a problem, for the impression it gives is that it is quoting scripture, but these words do not appear elsewhere in the Bible. The text that comes closest to it is Isaiah 40:1, but even in this case the quote is not direct. Probably the quote is taken, not from scripture, but from an ancient hymn—perhaps one that was sung at baptism.

In verse 15 the imagery changes, for now the contrast is between the wise and the unwise. This will continue as the central theme in the passage we will study tomorrow, up to verse 20. In today's text we see that the wise make good use of time, knowing that circumstances are not propitious ("the days are evil," 5:16).

Judge: In John 3:19 Jesus says that "the light has come into the world, and people loved darkness rather than light because their deeds were evil." Do you think this refers only to people who are not Christians? Or is it also true that we Christians hide things from one another because we fear that if they were known we would turn out to be less than we claim? Is this any different from "lying," which we studied sometime ago? Do you think the church would be a healthier body if, rather than hiding our faults, we were to help one another overcome them?

Take something else into consideration: If we truly believe that the light will triumph in the end, how is it that we still trust that the darkness will hide our sin? Hiding in the darkness, as if it could cover us forever, may well be a sign that we do not really trust the final victory of light.

Act: Imagine what your life would be if it were completely out in the open, so that all your actions and thoughts were known. Our first reaction to such a thought is one of fear. But when you think about it, you come to the conclusion that the less you have to hide the more you live in peace and joy. Consider the possibility of letting some of your trusted brothers and sisters in the church know you better. This will require that they learn some things about you that you have kept from them. It may be, however, that your life will be enriched.

Sixth Day: Read Ephesians 5:18-20.

See: This passage includes a contrast between those who are "drunk with wine" and those who are "filled with the Spirit." The unwise get "drunk with wine," whereas being "filled with the Spirit" characterizes the wise. This reminds us of the story of Pentecost, when those present thought the disciples, who were filled with the Spirit, were actually drunk.

This contrast is established because those who are drunk think and act differently than they would when they are sober. This is true both of those who are drunk with wine and of those who are "drunk" (filled) with the Spirit. Those who are drunk with wine lose common sense and decency and end in what the epistle calls "debauchery." Those who are drunk with the Spirit also leave behind the common way of thinking and acting. But instead of descending into debauchery, they ascend into what is described in verses 19 and 20.

Note that in these two final verses of our section for today, the subject is again words and speech. Practically all that is said there has to do with speaking, singing, making melody, and giving thanks. Once again we see the importance of words and speech.

Judge: The text deals with two realities that alter one's thoughts and behavior: wine and the Holy Spirit. In our society there seems to be an eager desire to escape from reality, especially among youth, but also among adults. Hence the popularity of the use of drugs that alter the mind. These include illegal drugs as well as alcohol and even sometimes prescription drugs.

The reason such drug use has become common is in part that the daily reality of many people leaves much to be desired. The daily grind, conflicts at home and at work, and lack of goals in life lead people to seek escape into some other reality. This they do by means of alcohol and drugs. Besides the obvious health consequences, drug and alcohol abuse is also tragic because people escape into a "reality" that is not real, but is even more false than the reality they sought to escape. This is what the epistle calls "debauchery."

But there is another reality. This too is beyond the daily and visible reality. It is the reality of the future that God has promised, of the day when the light shall overcome all darkness. Even though we cannot leap from our present reality to the promised one, we can have a foretaste of the latter. We can do this through the Spirit, who is the guarantee or down payment of that promise.

Thus, those who are filled with the Holy Spirit, even though still living in the daily reality that others seek to escape through drugs or alcohol, are in a way living also in the coming reality. That future order makes an impact on the present, so that those who are filled with the Spirit begin practicing even in the present life the goodness and truth that are to come to fruition in the future.

Act: Repeat the prayer from the second day of this week: "Thank you, our God, for the new life you have given us in Christ Jesus. Thank you, because we know there is nothing we have done or anything we could have done to deserve it. Help us behave as behooves that life, as children of light and not of darkness. We pray in the name of Jesus Christ, our life and our light. Amen."

Seventh Day: Read Ephesians 5:21-33.

See: Today's text is part of a longer passage that continues to Ephesians 6:9. When we look at it as a whole, it is clear that it is parallel to the passage in Colossians 3:18–4:1 that we studied earlier (and also to 1 Peter 2:17–3:7). As we saw in the case of Colossians, the passage deals with three unequal relationships: husbands and wives, fathers and children, masters and slaves. The fact that the three sets of relationships appear in these various documents has led some to suggest that this was a fairly common theme in the teachings of the early church.

Review what we have studied in the case of Colossians regarding the enormous power husbands had over their wives according to the Roman legal system. You will remember that a wife could not have property, except for a dowry that was managed by her husband. The husband had the right to divorce her with great ease, but she could not do likewise. Physical abuse of wives was fairly common and was not punished. In case of a divorce, the children as well as most of the property belonged to the husband.

The text we are studying is frequently used to tell women that they are to be subject to their husbands and do anything they command. The most often quoted verses are 22 and 23: "Wives, be subject to your husbands as you are to the Lord, for the husband is the head of the wife." On the basis of these verses, some have even claimed that the husband has the right to strike his wife.

What such interpretations forget is that this entire passage is part of a letter whose main theme is newness of life. For this reason, when we read it, the first question we must ask is what was it saying in its time that was really new. That the wives were to be subject to husbands (as well as children to their fathers and slaves to their masters) was nothing new. This was what all did, or at least were supposed to do. This was part of "the course of the world."

What the text says that is really new, first and above all, is that all are to be subject. Verse 21, which is the introduction to the entire section, is the radically new instruction: All are to be "subject to one another out of reverence for Christ." This sets the tone for the rest of the passage, which repeatedly tells the powerful, who are accustomed to commanding and having others subject to them, that they too are to be subject.

In verse 25 husbands are told that they are to love their wives as Christ loved the church and gave himself for her. This is a radically new thing to many. To tell husbands in the Roman Empire of the first century, accustomed as they were to do as they wished and even to abuse their wives, that they were to love their lives and even give up their lives for them was unheard of.

Note also that the central metaphor throughout the passage is that the church is the bride of Christ. This obviously means that Christ loves the church. But it also means that any arrogant husband listening to the reading of this letter was reminded that he was not only a husband. As part of the church, he also had a husband! His husband—the husband of the entire church, men as well as women—is Christ.

Therefore, this text, so often used to tell women to be subject to their husbands and even to justify physical and psychological abuse within marriage, is in fact radically opposed to such practices, telling husbands that they are to be subject to their wives, and that both men and women are to imitate Christ and be subject to him.

The radical element in this passage is that the epistle tells both the powerful and the powerless that they are to be subject. They are to be subject to each other.

Judge: You have probably heard that since Paul told wives "to be subject to your husbands as you are to the Lord" this means that they are to tolerate whatever their husbands say or do, and that husbands have the right to do and say whatever they wish. In the Latino tradition, sometimes in order to say that somebody got married, we say that they "had St. Paul read." The phrase reflects the custom of reading this passage at the wedding ceremony to remind the bride that she has to obey her new husband. But such an understanding of the epistle is not newness of life, but the reaffirmation of the old life and "the course of the world." The newness of life proposed here, the new relationship created by God's love, is to be found in verse 21: "Be subject to one another."

Why do you think we hear verse 22 quoted so much more often than verse 21? Could it be that many of us, in spite of all we say about the new life, are so rooted in the old, and in the customs and traditions that are part of our society and culture, that we are not ready to hear the Lord's radically new word?

Act: If you are married, ask your spouse to study this passage with you. In this study, make sure you pay close attention to verse 21. Discuss the meaning of being subject to each other. If in your conversation you decide that you have not practiced this full equality, discuss what steps are necessary to do so.

Whether you are married or not, there are near you many women who are physically or mentally abused by their husbands, even within the church. If your church is not using this material for group study, ask your pastor to read this section and then to conduct a study in church about marital abuse and its roots in incorrect interpretations of Scripture.

For Group Study

You may wish to look back at what you did as a group when studying the parallel passage in Colossians. It is important for the group to understand that, although today we study mostly relationships within marriage, the passage then moves on to other unequal relationships: fathers and children, masters and slaves.

Divide the group into teams of two. On each team, appoint one person to be husband, father, and master. Appoint another to be wife, child, and slave. (To force people to think radically about these matters, try to make sure that not only men play the role of husbands, and not only women act as wives.) When all have understood their role, explain the customs and laws of the time regarding each of these relationships. (See what has been said above, and also with reference to the parallel passage in Colossians.) Stress the inequality, the lack of all rights on the part of wives, children, and slaves.

Explain that in the ancient church, when a letter such as this was read, all would be present. These words were not read primarily by wives in private, nor even by a group of wives trying to discover their responsibilities. Such a letter would be read out loud in the meeting of the congregation. Therefore, wives would overhear what was being said to their husbands, and slaves would listen attentively to what was said to their masters.

Make sure that all understand clearly that they have to continue imagining the roles assigned to them. Now read the entire passage very slowly, continuing up to 6:9. After completing the reading, ask the "wives, children, and slaves" what impressed them most. Do likewise with the "husbands, fathers, and masters."

Most probably, what has been most surprising is not what was expected (for instance, that wives were to be subject to their husbands) but the radically new (for instance, that masters are to "do the same" to slaves as slaves do to them).

Make certain that part of the discussion revolves around the issue of marital abuse and what can be done against it.

W E E K
THIRTEEN

First Day: Read Ephesians 6:1-4.

See: Today's passage is the continuation of what we studied yesterday. Again, remember that there are parallel texts in Colossians and 1 Peter. These passages have usually been called "household legislation." As we have seen before, in order to understand their meaning we have to know something of the social context in which they were written, and how they would affect the lives of early Christians.

Having studied yesterday the section dealing with husbands and wives, we turn now to those having to do with fathers and children, and slaves and masters. Note that the first of these two pairs does not refer to "parents" and children. The reason is that the father had over his children an authority that the mother did not have—indeed, once the male children grew up, they might well have authority over their mother.

As an example of the absolute authority of a father, it may be good to repeat the ancient Roman custom declaring a child to be illegitimate until the father decided otherwise. The tradition was that the newborn was placed on the floor awaiting the father's entrance. If the father picked up the child this meant that he recognized it. If not, it was as if the child had never been born. It was left outdoors, exposed to the elements and to the beasts, until it died or was picked up by someone who would raise the child, perhaps as a slave or a prostitute.

As we read this passage with that context in mind, we see that here again, as in the case of husbands and wives, what is said about the obligation of the weak to obey the strong is not new.

What is new and even radical is that fathers are told that they do not have the right to treat their children as they wish. They are so to limit the exercise of their legal rights that the children are not provoked to anger, but rather are brought up "in the discipline and instruction of the Lord."

Judge: The purpose of the passage when it was written was to limit the power of fathers, who otherwise could oppress and abuse their children. There are places today where such abuse is practiced. Unfortunately, there are some who use this text to claim that a father has absolute authority over his children and can deal with them in any way he wishes. The result is that the death of children abused by their fathers is a daily occurrence.

What do you think the church should say about this? Is it possible to understand this text in such a way that it speaks against child abuse rather than for it?

If Paul wrote to a family today, what do you think he would say about this matter?

Act: If you are a father, think of how you are raising your children. Remember above all that you also have a Father, God. No matter who you are, think of what the text says regarding honoring one's parents. If your parents are alive, consider some action to honor them. If they are not, consider how you can honor their memory. If you have not spoken with your parents in some time, make an effort to do so as soon as possible.

Second Day: Read Ephesians 6:5-9.

See: The word that the NRSV translates as "slaves" may also mean "servants." Actually, for some time most modern versions translated the passage as referring to "servants." Presumably, this was because the translators felt that after the abolition of slavery it was more pertinent to speak of "servants." We no longer have slaves, but we do have servants. However, the NRSV is correct in preferring the word "slaves." The servants of old were not employees, as they are today. They practically were property. Therefore, the text actually refers to slavery and to the relationship between slaves and masters.

Note that, as in the case of the other pairs we have studied (husbands and wives, fathers and children), the text has little that is new to say to the slaves. What it recommends is what was expected of them if they were to avoid horrible consequences. But what the text says to the masters is indeed new. Masters are to deal with their slaves in the same way that slaves are to deal with their masters! And the basis for this is that they also have a Master: "knowing that whatever good we do, we will receive the same again from the Lord, whether we are slaves or free." Just as in chapter 5 husbands are told that, as members of the body of Christ, they too have a husband, so are the masters now told that they too have a Master.

Judge: Do you think these words in Ephesians imply that Christians ought to defend slavery? Certainly not! How is it then that there are those who use the earlier part of the same passage in order to insist on the unilateral submission of wives to their husbands, and even on the right of husbands and fathers to abuse their wives and children? If somehow we interpret the passage about slaves in such a way that it does not mean we should have slaves today, shouldn't we do the same with the entire section on "household legislation"?

Act: Review the material above until you are thoroughly familiar with it and understand it. Look around you, and you will probably find someone who has difficulty with the "household legislation" or even someone who thinks it justifies abuse. If so, after prayer, talk with this person about a different way to interpret this particular passage.

Third Day: Read Ephesians 6:10.

See: The word "finally" tells us that we are approaching the end of the epistle. After the doctrinal and inspirational sections in the early chapters, and the more practical advice in the latter ones, there is a final exhortation. This will be general in nature, but will prove valuable as a way to reinforce what the rest of the letter recommends.

This final exhortation, built around the metaphor of the "armor of God," begins in verse 10, which we shall study today. Paul's final exhortation is introduced in this one verse as a call to strength. Note that in scarcely two lines we have the words "strong," "strength," and "power."

Judge: If this is the first book of this series that you are following, you have spent almost three months (a little over twelve weeks) in a discipline of study and action. If this is not your first book in the series, you have been following this discipline for an even longer time. As we review this time, we discover that there are at least two ways in which we are strengthened.

The first is study and discipline. At the beginning of this study was a recommendation to set aside a time and a place for it. If you were able to do so, you will have come to a deeper understanding of the value and power of discipline. You set a discipline for yourself. Perhaps you were not always able to follow it, for life never follows strictly our schedules and plans. But even so, this discipline has helped you continue your study. It may even have brought more discipline to the rest of your life, for it is a common experience in devotional practice that it tends to spill out into the whole of life.

The second way in which we have probably been strengthened in our Christian life is the help and the support of others. This is the reason for the recommendation that if possible these studies be done by a group meeting once a week and also studying the same passages during the other six days of the week. But even if you were not able to do that, you will have discovered what John Wesley taught, that Christian life is never solitary. It is always life nourished in a community of faith.

Act: Review the notes you have written during the last twelve weeks. Have you been able to follow through with your discipline? Which of your resolutions did you follow, and which not?

Why were you able to follow up on some of them but not on others? Write your conclusions. Begin thinking about how you will continue your discipline of Bible study after you finish this book.

Fourth Day: Read Ephesians 6:11-12.

See: According to this text, Christian life is a struggle with opponents far beyond human ones (what the text calls "blood" and "flesh"). The struggle is rather "against the rulers, against the authorities, against the cosmic powers of this present darkness, against the spiritual forces of evil in the heavenly places." At least most of these are demonic powers. The "rulers" and "authorities" may be among such powers, or may be a reference to government. At any rate, when Ephesians speaks of such evil powers it is not referring to little devils flying around with pitchforks, as in popular mythology. It is actually declaring that evil is organized and makes alliances with rulers and other human realities. Paul himself had a long struggle, not just against some Jews who persecuted him or against a little devil tempting him, but against the entire power structure of Jerusalem and later of the Roman Empire.

Judge: This is why the text says that special strength is needed. Just as newness of life comes not from within ourselves, but from God, the strength necessary to continue in that life comes not from us, but from God. As you reviewed the resolutions in your notebook yesterday, did you find any that you were not able to follow because you imagined that you could do so on your own and then discovered that your strength and resolve were not enough?

If the struggle is not against flesh or blood, but against rulers and against cosmic powers, we need resources far beyond ourselves. It is to this that Paul refers when he speaks of the "armor of God," which we shall study tomorrow. Meanwhile, consider the possibility that this very discipline of study, prayer, and action that you have been following may be a way in which God helps you "stand against the wiles of the devil."

Act: Pray: "We thank you God, because although we know that our strength and resources are insufficient for the task, you do provide strength and resources. Teach us to trust in your strength rather than in ours, and help us stand firm against the wiles that will draw us away from you and your will. Amen."

Fifth Day: Read Ephesians 6:13-17.

See: The imagery here is of a Roman legionnaire ready for battle. The typical attire of such a soldier is "the whole armor" that the epistle takes as a model. The phrase "having done everything" means being totally prepared. Soldiers knowing that a battle was at hand would put on "the whole armor," which they would not wear all the time. Thus, the passage refers to the danger and urgency of battle. The exhortation to "fasten the belt of truth around your waist" would remind readers of the thick belt that a legionnaire usually wore. The "breastplate of righteousness" may be a reference to Isaiah 59:17.

Legionnaires usually wore light shoes that allowed them to move with both speed and endurance. Christians are to "proclaim the gospel of peace," which implies that they are messengers of the Great King. This reference to "shoes for your feet" reminds us of Paul's words in Romans 10:15 regarding those who proclaim the gospel of peace, whose feet he declares to be beautiful.

The "shield of faith" refers to the special shield that Roman soldiers used against archers. It was a wooden shield covered with hide, about four feet high and three feet wide. When the archers attacked, all the legionnaires would raise their shields so that they would touch each other, providing protection both around and above the soldiers, in a formation called "the tortoise." The archers would shoot flaming arrows, but these were unable to penetrate the shell that the legionnaires had built with their large shields.

The helmet protected the head, which was subject to the most dangerous blows. The Christian soldier's best defense against such blows is in remembering his or her own salvation and the power behind it. This is why the epistle calls its readers to "take the helmet of salvation."

Up to this point, only defensive weapons are mentioned. They are instruments for the soldier's protection against the enemy. But now the epistle refers to "the sword of the Spirit, which is the word of God." A sword is both a defense and an offensive weapon. A good soldier uses it not only to stop the enemy's thrusts, but also to attack. Therefore, the struggle to which the text refers is not only a matter of defense. Christians are not only to remain firm against the enemy that attacks them, but are also to take the offensive against that enemy.

Judge: This passage used to be very popular but has been criticized more recently for its militaristic tone. There is no doubt that militarism—the notion that all can be solved by force of arms—is to be rejected. Each day, militarism uses up resources that could be better employed feeding and providing shelter for millions who are hungry and homeless.

But the truth is that the passage does not defend militarism. What it actually says is that Christian life is as dangerous as that of any soldier. This is both true and important. Some people, perhaps in order to avoid sounding militant, refuse to acknowledge the seriousness of the struggle. This leads to a comfortable sort of Christianity, which tends to equate being a Christian with being a decent person, meeting one's social obligations, and having the respect of others. However, if it is true that being a true believer involves a new life, and dying to the old, things are different. Christians who are convinced of this should expect "the course of the world" to oppose them. Given such great opposition, it is important to be protected by "the whole armor of God."

Imagine thousands of soldiers marching against an enemy. The enemy attacks them with thousands of arrows, many of them burning. The soldiers immediately raise their shields and build a shell as impenetrable as a tortoise shell.

Such a defense works if all do their part and work together. But if each runs in a different direction, if some attack, others retreat, and others hesitate, they will have little or no defense against the enemy's arrows.

Something similar is true regarding the Christian life. The enemy is launching "flaming arrows" against us. These come from different directions, and often several at once. There is no way we can protect ourselves from such an attack. If we raise our shield in one direction, the enemy will attack us from the other. But if, instead of responding individually, we all protect one another, the arrows of the enemy will be kept at bay.

Here are some examples. A brother is disillusioned about something, and his faith wavers. If he seeks to stand alone, he will fall. But if he is surrounded by people who encourage and support him, the outcome will be different. A sister is tempted by a well-paying but questionable job. If she does not have others with whom to discuss her options and measure the consequences, she may well succumb to temptation. Can you think of other examples, perhaps out of your own experience?

Act: Make a list in your notebook of people on whom you can count to support you and your faith in difficult times. Try to think of such times and how these people have helped you, perhaps as so many legionnaires surrounding you with their shields. Resolve that you will be available when they need you. End your study session by praying for them.

Sixth Day: Read Ephesians 6:18-20.

See: Yesterday we dealt with a series of weapons in our struggle against the powers of evil. Today's text adds something we should never forget: the best weapon Christians can use to protect one another is prayer. In verse 19 it is a matter of prayer "for all the saints." In verses 19 and 20 Paul asks his readers to pray for him.

Throughout these studies we have repeatedly noted that one of the fundamental elements of the new life is a new community. The new life in Christ is life in community. The church is part of the good news. It is there that we find strength and support in order to live out the good news. Likewise, the Christian struggle against evil is not a private matter for each Christian, but is a matter of community. And one of the ways in which the church is united and its members support one another even when they are apart is intercessory prayer.

Note also that, as before, Paul asks his readers to pray not that he may be freed, but rather that he may be able to proclaim "the mystery of the gospel" and that he may do it "boldly." Speaking "boldly" is a subject that appears also in Acts 4:15, 29, and 31. There it creates difficulties for the apostles, who still insist on doing it. Now Paul himself asks his readers to pray that he may speak "boldly," even though that is not likely to sit well with the authorities who have him in prison.

Judge: Do you pray often for your brothers and sisters in the faith? If there is a group of you following this study, have you been supporting one another in prayer, especially on the days you do not gather?

Do you think the church would be any different if its members truly and earnestly prayed for one another more often?

Act: Pray, using the following words as a guide. Note that although you are praying alone, you are using plural pronouns, for you are praying in the name of the whole church:

"We thank you, Lord, that although the struggle is difficult you give us ever renewed strength. We thank you for the armor that you provide us. We thank you particularly for the shield of faith that keeps us from the flaming arrows of evil. Give us wisdom and guidance to use it, not only for our own defense, but also for the defense of others. We ask this in the name of Jesus Christ, in whom you have already given us victory. Amen."

Seventh Day: Ephesians 6:21-24.

See: Tychicus is the bearer of this letter, as he was also (jointly with Onesimus) of the epistles to the Colossians and Philemon. (On the significance of Tychicus, remember what was said above in the third day of the seventh week.) Paul sends him with the letter so that he can give his readers direct and personal news regarding Paul and his companions. As was then customary, it is probable that the purpose of this letter is to serve as an introduction for Tychicus, who would have more to say to the addressees in Paul's name. Today, instead of such a long letter, we simply write a brief note of introduction, and sometimes even write the note on a visiting card.

When we first read these last verses of the letter, we are inclined not to pay them too much attention. After all, it is a series of greetings among people we do not know. But if we remember how the letter insists on the need for unity and mutual love, and how Christians ought to pray for one another, we realize that these last verses are a fundamental part of the letter, for what they do is to act out much of what the letter itself recommends.

Tychicus is to bear news from Paul and his companions because they are part of the church, and so are the addressees. In order to foster their sense of community they have to keep in contact. Distance might weaken the unity of the church, but Paul avoids this by keeping people in touch with one another and in prayer for one another.

Judge: "How large is your church?" Many of us, when we hear such a question, think in terms of our local congregation and answer, for instance, "My church is small, for we have only forty members," or "My church is large, for we have several thousand members."

It is certainly good that when we think about the church the first thing that comes to mind is the concrete community with which we gather to worship. The church is precisely these people who worship with us.

But the church is much more than that. The question *How large is your church?* should also be considered in a different way. It is a matter not only of how many members there are in your local congregation, but also of how encompassing is your vision of the church.

Paul, a prisoner, probably in Rome, is thinking about the churches in Colossae, in Philippi, and elsewhere. About what and whom do we think when we try to visualize the church?

In other words, does your "church" include other congregations of your own denomination nearby? Does it include the entire denomination? Does it include other denominations? Does it include people in other ages? When you think about the church, do you also include the church in China, in Ethiopia, in Cyprus? Do you remember "all the saints who from their labors rest"? When you pray for fellow Christians in difficult situations, do you remember the church in the Sudan, in North Korea, and in Iran? Do you pray for Protestants, Catholics, Orthodox, Pentecostals, and others?

Ask once again, *How big is my church?*

Act: Paul sends greetings and requests news from churches in other parts of the world. Do the same. Resolve to learn how your sisters and brothers in other parts of the world live and pray, and what challenges they face. Remember the example of the ancient Roman legionnaires, all raising their shields to protect one another. Only if believers in all nations and of all denominations understand one another will they be able to help one another, as those soldiers of old.

Find a book that talks about the life of believers in other places or times. Read it as you would the story of relatives with whom you have not had recent contact. Ask your pastor to help you learn more about the many aspects of world Christianity. Pray for all these relatives you have had for so long and are just discovering.

For Group Study

Close this session by stressing what is probably the main point of all we have studied during these three months: Christian life is a life of joy in the midst of tribulation—Philippians. It is a life that encompasses all things in the service of the Lord of all—Colossians. It is such a radically new life that it is as if we had died to the old life—Colossians and Ephesians. But it is not an easy life. It is a life of struggle against the power of the old self, of death, and of evil.

In this new life our supreme resource is the strength we receive from God. But God also gives us means of defense, and the most important of these is the community of the faithful. We must therefore defend one another and pray for one another.

As you reach the end of these three months of study, invite the group to make a formal commitment before God and one another to pray for and to support one another in the faith.

Reserve the last five or ten minutes for discussing how you are to continue a discipline of Bible study.

Finally, ask the group to remember in their prayers their brother in the faith who has written these lines. May God bless you and keep you!